TAROT IN ACTION!

Practical examples of different spreads, how to read them and how to develop Tarot-reading skills.

TAROT IN ACTION!

An introduction to simple and more complex Tarot spreads

by

SASHA FENTON

THE AQUARIAN PRESS

First published 1987

10 9 8 7 6 5 4

British Library Cataloguing in Publication Data

Fenton, Sasha
  Tarot in action!: an introduction to
  simple and more complex Tarot spreads.
  1. Tarot (Game)
  I. Title
  795.4   GV1295.T37

  ISBN 0-85030-525-X

*The Aquarian Press is part of the Thorsons Publishing Group,
Denington Estate, Wellingborough, Northamptonshire, NN8 2RQ, England*

Printed and bound by R. Clay Limited, Bungay, Suffolk

DEDICATION

This book is dedicated with much affection to the Knight of Cups in person, Simon Franklin.

Fortuna Imperatrix Mundi

(Luck, Empress of the World)

Fortune rota volvitur:
descendo minoratus;
alter in altum tollitur;
nimis exaltatus

(The wheel of chance spins:
one man is abased by its descent;
the other is carried aloft;
all too exalted)

From *Carmina Burana* by Carl Orff.

CONTENTS

INTRODUCTION

Every new deck of Tarot cards has a leaflet tucked into its packet. This gives the potential Tarot Reader a brief introduction to the meaning of each card and it may also show one or two methods of spreading the cards. This, obviously, does not take the student very far, so the next step is to buy a book which gives a fuller explanation of the cards. There are many of these books around; my own book, *Fortune-telling by Tarot Cards*, is specially designed for the beginner.

Even after reading a couple of these books and trying out a few readings, the student will still find it difficult to give a reading with confidence. What he or she needs at that point is to get together with an experienced Reader and to watch him at work. If the experienced Reader is inclined to be helpful — and the majority of them are — he will tell the student how and why he reaches his conclusions from the cards in front of him. This would be rather like an apprentice watching a craftsman at work. The apprentice will find his own style of working as he develops his skills, but those early examples could be just the thing to break the ice and bring the subject to life. In this book, I am playing the part of the craftsman and allowing the apprentice Reader to peek over my shoulder and see how I have come to my conclusions.

All Tarot Readers are idiosyncratic, and in many cases the Tarot cards are used primarily as a focus for clairvoyance. Therefore, one could argue that each potential Reader has to find *his own way* of giving a reading and his own way of setting out the cards. He may eventually become so clairvoyant that he ends up putting the cards back into their box and doing all his readings from mental images in his head. For those who have not reached these dizzy heights of perspicacity, a bit of help will do no harm.

I have learned a trick or two myself since writing my previous Tarot book, and any useful ideas which I omitted from that book or have since discovered, have been included in this one. These ideas are tucked in and around the sample readings as well as being in the strictly informative chapters.

I have chosen twelve different layouts in this book with variations on some of them. This is to give a broad selection of possible methods. I have tried to choose a cross-section of people for the readings with a variation of lifestyle, interests and problems. However, most people are interested in relationships, money and work, and these themes crop up time and time again, however much I search for something different. It seems that our prehistoric need for survival is still paramount to us and this shows up in the form of security, money and work (mostly the male Questioners) and security, money and relationships (mostly the female Questioners).

Of all the problems that people can have, health problems are the worst because there is not too much that a sick person can do to change his circumstances. Relationships are always difficult because one is trying to make another person feel, behave and even perhaps *be* what he or she cannot. Children can wind their parents up to a pitch of anger and guilt at the drop of a hat — elderly parents can do so even more quickly. To be honest, the longer the student studies the Tarot, philosophy and people, the sooner he will see that we are all much the same. I am sure that the average African witch-doctor could show us that his clients ask the same questions and have the same basic requirements as the most sophisticated Londoner. Perhaps the Russians, Chinese and Americans should learn to read each others' Tarot cards — they will find to their surprise that the desire for good health, a reasonable position in one's peer group and the need for love, comfort and family life are pretty universal.

There is no specific, correct or authorized way of reading Tarot cards. Even the British Astrological and Psychic Society, an organization which assesses Readers for professional status, does not question the methods used; they only measure the accuracy of the reading.

A skilled Reader will adapt the interpretation of a card to each new reading, but the beginner should start with the standard Tarot meanings and work from there. In some of the spreads I have demonstrated the use of the cards in both the upright and the reversed positions; in other spreads, I have used all the cards in the upright position. In most spreads I have used a mixture of Major and Minor Arcana cards, but I have demonstrated a couple of spreads twice, using only the Major Arcana for the second Questioner's reading. One final note on the subject of technique: when making general comments I use the terms 'he' and 'him', in order to save the text from becoming laboured.

ACKNOWLEDGEMENTS

It is simply not possible for one Tarot Reader, however experienced, to have gained enough knowledge for a book like this. I have spent a lot of time discussing Tarot with my many friends and colleagues, both professional and amateur, and would like to thank not only those who have given me information especially for this book, but also those whose tips over the years have proved themselves to be valuable.

Douglas and Nina Ashby
Simon Franklin
Barbara Ellen Narbeth
Roy Sinclair
Jean Goodey
Bethany Lyne-Pirkis
Malcolm Wright
David Talfryn
James Haslam
Vicki Lester

Margaret Rae
Joan Jackson
Lars Bratt
Bernard Stringer
David and Eve Bingham
Tina Artemis
Gordon Smith
Janis Huntley
Renee Hindle
Fred Curtis

Thanks also to my husband Tony and my children Helen and Stuart for their help, to Kay Bielecki for proof-reading, and to Anne Christie for tips on writing and for encouraging me when my spirit was flagging.
Also thanks to all those who acted as 'guinea-pigs' for this book.

CHAPTER ONE

General Information

Choice of spread

Very few Tarot readers question themselves as to why they rely on a particular group of spreads. If someone were to ask them to give a reason for their choice, they would probably say that they use spreads which 'feel right'. Tarot is an instinctive, intuitive art and it is not in the nature of Readers to subject their methods to close analysis; however, for the sake of this book, I have set my mind to discovering the relative values of different spreads.

Spreads seem to fall into three groups, the first being the *comprehensive* group which is used to give a generalized reading. This not only gives a wealth of information but also allows the cards to show the Reader where the Questioner's most pressing problems and decisions lie. The second group are the *focused* spreads, which you can use in order to take a close look at one specific question. It is best to use one of these after completing a comprehensive type of reading in order to close in on one or two of the events which have shown themselves to be important.

Finally, there are the *calendar* spreads. These are used to give a reading for a specific length of time ahead. This spread can also be used to find out *when* a particular event is going to occur, for instance if a client wants to know when he is going to move house, a six, eight or ten week ahead spread could be used with cards relevant to house moves being borne in mind.

Tarot is a pathway which can be used alone or in conjunction with astrology, numerology or the Kabbala. I have demonstrated readings myself which combine Tarot and astrology while my friend, Douglas

Ashby, has demonstrated a reading based on Tarot and the Kabbala for which we used the familiar Tree of Life spread. It is worth experimenting with some of these concepts but, to be honest, it is best to be familiar with the concepts of astrology or the Kabbala in the first place, as then one has only the cards to worry about. Remember, each person works in a slightly different manner. Both Douglas and I have followed, in most cases, the commonly known Tarot interpretations, but having one reading demonstrated by a number of different Readers adds just a touch of spice.

Each reading carries with it an element of healing. Even when a Questioner is having the reading for amusement or to satisfy his curiosity, he will derive benefit from sitting quietly alongside the Reader. A Questioner who is troubled will often feel better after a reading and there are three good reasons for this. Firstly, the reading might be enlightening — it could well be useful to know just what is around the corner. Secondly, immediately after the reading the Questioner usually chats for a while, benefiting from the chance to talk things over confidentially with a detached outsider. The third benefit comes from the very act of receiving a reading; this is because there is always a measure of psychic 'giving out' involved with any reading, which encourages a flow of relaxing and healing waves to wash over the Questioner. Readers and Questioners invariably sit close together because both of them are usually looking at the cards. It is worth mentioning at this point that if the Reader suspects that he or she is particularly susceptible to psychic disturbances, he should not sit directly opposite the Questioner but should place himself in a side-ways-on position. This is to protect the chakra centres* from harmful influences.

This book is about *divination* by the Tarot, but it can also be used for meditation purposes. The simplest method is for the beginner to select a card, look at the picture and then put the card down while retaining the image in the mind. Then let the mind drift with the image changing and developing as in a daydream.

Lastly, and probably most importantly, one must make a point of

---

* Chakra centres: seven imaginary psychic openings in the body which allow energies to flow in and out.

'closing down' after any kind of psychic work. If you are familiar with the chakra centres, then close them one by one in the way in which you have been taught. If this is all Greek to you, then I suggest that you use this method which was passed on to me by my friend David Bingham, who is a professional psychic. Pretend that you are climbing into a sleeping bag, imagine that you are pulling it up over your head and then tying it up on the top of your head. If you don't do something to close down after any kind of psychic work then you will find it hard to get to sleep and may pick up other people's feelings of depression, or even their ailments! This is called collecting psychic garbage (or even worse).

So read on and then try out some of these ideas, always remembering that your own ideas and feelings are right, even if they are totally different from mine.

Ratios

It is a good idea with any large spread to take a look at the ratio of one kind of card to another. It is not necessary to make a big production out of counting up the different kinds of cards in the spread, just a glance to see if the layout is *dominated* by any one group of cards.

Here are some ratio ideas which I have set out for you in a descending order of importance.

1. Every deck of Tarot cards contains twenty-two Major Arcana cards and fifty-six Minor Arcana cards; therefore a spread should have a rough ratio of two Minor Arcana cards to each Major Arcana card. If there are significantly more Major then Minor cards, events will tend to be in the hands of fate, whereas if the cards are mainly Minor Arcana, then matters are more likely to be in the hands of the Questioner himself.
2. If there are more than two or three Court cards, the Questioner will be surrounded by and influenced by many people.
3. A high proportion of Staves indicates an emphasis on communication and negotiations.
4. Mainly Cups indicates that the emphasis is on the emotional side of life.

5. Mainly Swords shows that swift and decisive action will be required, possibly due to unexpected problems.
6. Mainly Coins shows that the accent is on property, business, financial and security matters.

Ritual and procedure

I have gone into this at length in my previous book, but I will give a brief résumé of those ideas again here. Firstly, keep your Tarot cards safe and don't use them to play card games with. They can be kept in silk, if you like, as this is supposed to enhance their psychic powers and keep evil forces away from them. I have always kept my cards in a box, but it's a matter of personal preference.

Secondly, be careful not to frighten a Questioner. If the reading looks really black, then tone your interpretation down, as it is better to lose some credibility than to upset anyone too much. Be honest, but take some of the sharp edges off your interpretation.

Thirdly, there are various ways of shuffling and dealing the cards. You can give the cards to the Questioner and ask him to shuffle, then cut the cards into three. Ideally, he should do this with his left hand, moving the cut cards to the left, but it honestly doesn't matter that much. You can reverse one of the three decks if you like, or you can leave the cards as they are and use them all in the upright position. If you want to choose a significator, do this before the Questioner shuffles the cards. Cards can be dealt from the top of the pile or spread out face down in a rough line, with the Questioner picking the required number of cards at random. This will vary according to the type of reading which you are doing and also the mood you are in.

It is interesting to note which pile the Questioner chooses. The vast majority of people choose the middle pile. These are, for the most part, ordinary middle-of-the-road people who want the usual things out of life. If the cards have been placed at a slight angle or distance from the Questioner, he or she may choose the nearest pile, showing that he or she is reasonable, sensible, but maybe a touch lazy. The subject who chooses the one which is furthest away seems to want to go out on a limb. This person thinks along unconventional lines, is prepared to make strenuous efforts, and is never going to be content with second best.

For a reading using upright and reversed cards

The Questioner cuts the cards into three decks
and then chooses one of them.

The Reader turns the deck which the Questioner has chosen.

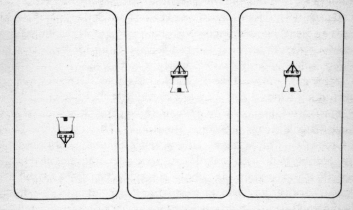

The end which was nearest to the Questioner must be placed nearest
to the Reader.

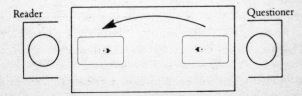

Synthesis

Once the student has picked up some idea of the meaning of the cards and looked at a few spreads, he then often finds himself looking down at a table full of contradictory or even unrelated cards and trying to make some sense of it all. The ability to match a bunch of cards to the Questioner's story is called 'synthesizing'.

The only suggestion which I can give at this point is to use your imagination. What you have to do, in a strange sort of way, is to find the common factor among the bunch of cards in front of you. If the book definitions don't quite fit but are not too far away, then change your wording a little to make the cards fit the story. If the cards refuse to relate to the subject which you want to focus upon — for instance, if you want to look at finances and the cards which have been chosen appear to be directed towards emotional matters — then tell the story which the cards *do* want to focus upon; you can always try another reading a bit later on. If nothing seems to relate at all, then allow your mind to drift a little and almost *make up* a story to fit the situation. This is not a case of hoodwinking your Questioner, or of ducking out of the whole idea of learning Tarot; it is giving your intuition, psychic powers, spirit guides etc., the chance to get going.

Let me give you a couple of practical examples. I have my deck of cards in my hands; I shall now try to estimate the state of health of an imaginary Questioner by drawing three cards at random. Okay, I have drawn the Page of Swords, the Knight of Staves and the Three of Coins. Well, these three cards *all* relate to a move of house and have nothing to do with health! If this were a genuine reading, I would immediately abandon the whole subject of health and tell the Questioner that the cards were far more interested in the possibility of a move of house. I would then continue with a fuller spread, confining my reading to the events leading up to, surrounding and following a house move.

I now have another go at the health problem with another three cards. This time I have the Two of Coins, the Ten of Coins and the Five of Cups. This could look like a move which although financially rewarding is emotionally draining, therefore the health of our imaginary subject would be weakened both by the effort of moving and by the sense of sadness and regret surrounding such a move. At this point, I would probably ask if the Questioner were leaving a spouse, or even leaving behind a working arrangement and moving to another place. I would be most surprised if the answer were a categorical 'no'.

A strange thing has just happened. It has just occurred to me that, immediately before sitting down to write this passage, I had been speaking to a friend who is drawing towards the end of a difficult relationship. Her health is not good at the moment and she knows that she will have to move out and find somewhere to live soon. She also works from home, so moving will affect her livelihood. Is this a coincidence? Or are we once again witnessing the magical Tarot at work?

CHAPTER TWO

Some of Your Questions Answered

I am often asked 'What do you do if you see something bad?' Sometimes I ask what is meant by 'bad', and the reply is invariably, 'Oh, death or maybe some terrible accident'. Well, there is no easy reply to this but there are a number of points to think about.

Firstly there is very little chance that a Reader would see the death of the Questioner himself. I have only on two occasions been aware that a client was actually dying at the time of the reading, and in each case the client herself was aware of it. I think that is the key to the situation: we are meant to help our clients to *solve* their problems, and it is not our place to *create* problems for them, especially insoluble ones like death. If a client comes to a Reader already *aware* that he or she is dying, there is something which can be given in the form of a sympathetic listening ear.

We often foresee death of persons who are around the Questioner and sometimes we can point out the relationship but, in practically every case that I have dealt with, the client was aware that the relative or friend in question was nearing the end of his or her life. Having said all that, if you are in any doubt then say nothing, water the reading down. It's better to lose two pennyworth of your credibility than to upset someone unnecessarily.

If you see events such as potential accidents, business losses, marital upsets etc., then use tact, common sense and a sympathetic attitude. Imagine how *you* would like to be told of hard times to come. By all means encourage people to face up to their problems, but do so kindly and tactfully. Don't try to gloss over bad news, but don't harp on it either. Try to give a balanced reading based on the Questioner's true situation both at the time of the reading and into the future. Even if the reading is a truly sad one, make a point of looking for happy future events, success and progress ahead. Life is never all doom and gloom and nothing lasts forever, not even bad times. Be realistic though; false optimism is not much help.

One question which I am occasionally asked is where my 'power' comes from. One curious thing about this question is that it is always asked by rather earnest young men! It seems apparent that these young men have strong religious views and are trying hard to please their local religious leaders and prove themselves to be good. I have no objection to these people or to their questions, but I have no answer for them. The truth is that neither I, nor any other Tarot Reader, has any magical powers. Anyone can become a Reader — it just takes practice. OK, I'll admit that some people make better Readers than others, just as some people are better at kicking a football than others, and I'll bet that nobody asks them where *their* power comes from.

Leading on from this question is the one which goes, 'Do you have to be someone special or can anyone read Tarot?' The answer is that anyone can learn to read the cards assuming that they a) can remember the meanings of the cards, b) have a certain amount of intuition, and c) are interested in other people. And it is the third part of this which is the most important, because so many people want to learn only in order to read for themselves. This may give them a few hours of fun but won't turn them into a skilled Reader.

A common remark is, 'I've heard that it's unlucky to do it for oneself.' The answer is that it is not even remotely unlucky to read the cards for oneself; however there are a couple of drawbacks. Firstly, you cannot give yourself — or anyone close to you for that matter — an *objective* reading, as your vision is always clouded by knowing too much about the situation. Secondly, after a few readings the cards start to contradict themselves and eventually send out nothing but garbage. I don't know why this happens, it just does. Even when I am reading for a client there comes a point, usually when I have completed three or four spreads, when their story starts to repeat itself and I know that there will be nothing more on this occasion. I think that the main reason for most people's failure to get a decent reading for themselves is that the cards are not meant to be a vehicle for self-indulgence, they are meant to be used for growth, awareness and to help others. Frankly, if you don't wish to put yourself out for others, to spend a part of your life concentrating on people and things outside of yourself, you won't have too much success with the Tarot.

People ask me 'How does it work? How can a few cards chosen at random tell anyone what is going to happen?' I don't really know the answer to this. I think that the cards probably work on the subconscious mind of the Reader. A great deal of information must be passed on along an invisible psychic wavelength.

Another question is 'How long does it take to learn the Tarot?' My answer is vague because some people take longer than others. Learning the meanings of the cards will be quicker if you have an agile and well-used brain. If you have not studied anything for the past thirty years and are not used to philosophical modes of thinking you will have problems. If you want to read the cards clairvoyantly, that is without knowing the specific meaning of each card, then I suggest a few months of clairvoyant training at a local development circle, healing circle or at the local Spiritualist church.

It took me three months to become familiar with the Tarot, but my method of learning was both unusual and rather outrageous. I was already working as an astrologer and palmist and simply explained to my clients that I was studying Tarot and offered them a free Tarot reading in addition to their other readings. I didn't get one refusal. People are most cooperative if they know what you are trying to do and if they feel secure in their minds that they are not being ripped off. After three months of this, I felt competent enough to begin charging for the readings. Now, I do far more Tarot readings than any other kind of readings, simply because it is quick and easy in comparison to astrology or palmistry, although in some cases the other two skills are more useful.

Another poser is 'If you did the reading over again, would it come out the same?' The answer is *yes*, it would. The cards would repeat the theme, the events of the past, present and future. They may lean towards family rather than work, or vice versa, but the same story would emerge. In too many cases for comfort a high proportion of the same cards appear, even in the same positions in the spread.

CHAPTER THREE

The Simplest Kind of Spread

The Choose-it-Yourself Spread

I invented this spread myself some years ago in order to introduce beginners to the idea of *applying* the cards to something rather than just drawing cards at random and trying to make sense out of them. The Reader has to ask the Questioner to choose six categories; these may be specific areas of his life or things which are particularly important to him at the time of the reading. This gives a lot of help to the Reader because it puts the onus on the Questioner to state what is on his mind, rather than leaving the poor Reader to fish around trying to work out what the Questioner's problems might be. Even professional readers sometimes use variations upon this idea by asking the Questioner to put three or four questions to the Reader. This is especially useful when the Reader has little time to spare.

Below are all the categories which I can remember having to deal with when demonstrating this spread.

Relationships	Health
Home and family	Travel
Parents	Spiritual pathway
Children	Holidays
Work	Sports and hobbies
Money	The family pet

Any number of categories can be chosen, but I find that six is a comfortable number. The Reader can take one, two or more cards for each category. I think that the most successful approach is to choose

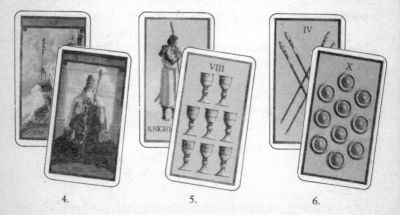

two cards and then elaborate on any category which seems to be especially interesting. A good method of elaboration is to use the two cards for the category in question and then work a seven-card 'consequences' spread over the top of them.

Roy

Roy is a pleasant young man who has a secure job as a commercial artist working in the armed services. He admits to having no problems in his life at present, although he has had some quite severe spells of illness over the past few years. Indeed, he still has to watch his health somewhat. He would like to find a steady girlfriend, although he doesn't feel that he is ready for marriage yet. He feels that he will come out of the forces in the not too distant future, but is not sure when or why.

Categories chosen by Roy:

1. Romance
2. Short-term career
3. Long-term career
4. Family (parents & sister)
5. Health
6. Money

For this reading, I asked Roy to shuffle and cut the cards and then to pick six pairs which I used in the upright position.

1. Five of Coins & Two of Staves
2. The High Priestess & Ace of Swords
3. Judgement & Queen of Swords
4. The Emperor & the Hierophant
5. Knight of Staves & Eight of Cups
6. Four of Staves & Ten of Coins

The reading

Position 1:
'You have chosen romance for your first category, the cards are the Five of Coins and the Two of Staves. This appears at first to be a peculiar mixture because the Five of Coins seems such a sad card due to its

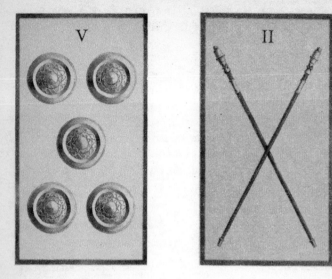

feeling of being left out in the cold, but in fact when applied to romance it's not a bad card to choose. The rather wretched feelings associated with this card apply mainly to money, business and other losses of a material nature; as far as love is concerned, it shows that there will be some light-hearted and pleasant romantic involvements in the near future. The other card is the Two of Staves and this, like all twos, implies partnership matters, but this will be on a social and conversational level rather than on a more intense, passionate level. Therefore, in the immediate future, probably two or three young ladies will keep you company but there will be nothing heavy.'

'I'd rather have a steady girlfriend but obviously that's not to be the case yet,' said Roy.

Position 2:
'This is your short-term career situation and here we find the High Priestess and the Ace of Swords. This implies that you may have to go on a course which could come up rather suddenly; this is because the Priestess implies teaching or learning. There certainly will be new projects soon and new methods to become used to. There could be

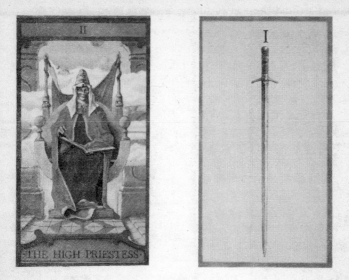

a connection with engineering through the Sword card but I am getting a clairvoyant picture in my head which tells me that you soon could be involved in some kind of photographic processes. Things will change quickly for you within your job and you will have to follow your intuition about any changes.'

'I can't see anything new going on at the moment, but these things do happen from time to time,' Roy agreed.

Position 3:
'We are now looking at your long-term career prospects and you have drawn the Judgement card and the Queen of Swords which shows me that you will not remain for ever in the forces. The Judgement card indicates an ending with some kind of reward or bonus payment and the Queen makes me think that a woman may be involved in your decision to come out; this could be the lady that you choose to marry. The severe nature of the Queen of Swords shows that you will not make any decisions about leaving the job and/or marrying without a lot of thought.'

'That seems to fit,' said Roy. 'I will be coming to the end of a three-year stint at around the age of thirty; it seems to fit the picture.'

Position 4:

'This represents your family and you have drawn the Emperor and the Hierophant which seem to be your parents. The Emperor would indicate a man of authority who is in charge of some business venture, so I assume that refers to your Dad. The Hierophant is, on the one hand, a spiritual card and also a card of tradition and marriage, therefore I think this represents your mother. I guess that she would be a very spiritual person and very much dedicated to your father. You say you have a sister, it is possible that she is getting married soon, this card would show that. Without pulling out further cards, I cannot tell you any more about your family at the moment, but these cards are good ones as they imply stability, therefore you could expect your family's affairs to remain much the same over the next few years.'

'My father manages a shop and until recently my mother had her own little shop, so they are both business people. Mother *is* devoted to Dad although they squabble all the time, and my sister is getting married later on this year!' said Roy.

Position 5:

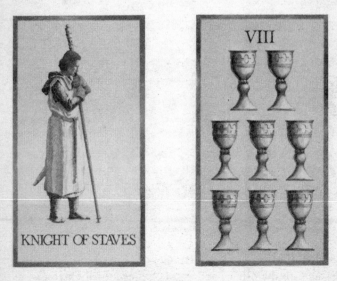

'This position represents health and here we have the Knight of Staves and the Eight of Cups. The Eight is the important card here as it implies that you are turning your back on the bad times of the past and moving forward to better times. There is an element of moving through a dark valley, therefore I expect you have been seriously ill in the past but the future looks better. The Knight is a card of movement and is hard to apply to health matters, so the only thing I can say is that you will not be *restricted* by poor health from now on. The Knight is telling you to travel about and see friends and not to worry too much. Neither of the cards indicates more trouble to come, but the Eight tells me that you still have to be careful for a little longer.'

'That's right, I am much better now but I do get twinges from time to time.'

Position 6:
'You have chosen this position to represent money, and for this you have picked the Four of Staves and the Ten of Coins. On one level

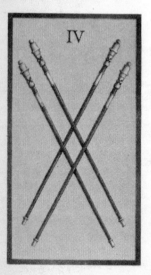 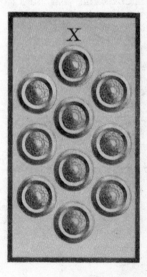

it could imply that you will come into money (the Ten) through property (the Four), but on the other hand you could eventually invest what you have in some property. It does indicate stable finances as both the Four, which implies putting down roots, and the Ten, which always means the start of something lasting, show that you will be quite well established financially in the future and should not be without money in years to come.'

'Obviously that's too far in the future for me to judge, but if it works out that way, I'll be very pleased,' said Roy.

After the reading
Roy asked me for more information about the girl he would be likely to marry, so we put the cards back and started again, this time using a Celtic Cross spread. The first card to emerge after the significator was the Queen of Swords. That has got to represent Roy's future wife.

CHAPTER FOUR

Focused Spreads

The Consequences Spread

This small spread is obviously most useful for answering a specific question. There are many ideas which are based on this spread as it is so flexible. The Reader can adapt the spread in many different ways to suit the requirements of each reading. The following spread designation is particularly useful for straightforward questions.

1. The person or situation.
2. Matters affecting the person or situation.
3. The past.
4. The future.
5. Suggested course of action.
6. Outside factors.
7. Consequence.

Variations can be achieved by using the cards in the upper area of the spread as the present and those at the bottom as the future; alternatively, one can use those on the left as the past and those on the right as the future. If a Court card shows up on the right, for instance, the card immediately above or below it can be used to find out more about the person who is being represented by the Court card.

Helen
Helen is a pretty young woman of twenty whose flashing dark eyes and masses of thick dark-brown hair give her a gipsyish appearance. She wanted to have a quick reading because she had just changed her

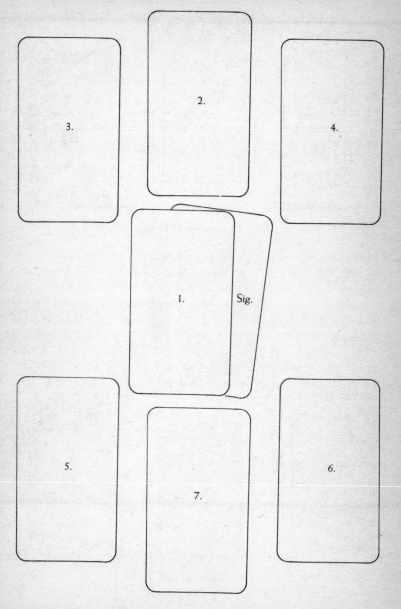

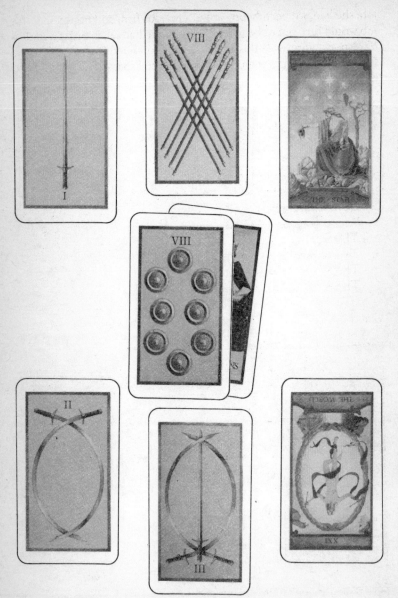

job: she had not been happy at her previous firm and hoped that this job would turn out to be more pleasant. She had taken on a good deal of responsibility with this new job and wondered if she could cope with it. We used my standard 'consequences' spread and went round the pattern twice.

After finding the significator from within the deck, I gave the cards to Helen and suggested that she shuffle them then spread them out along the table and select seven.

First spread
Significator, Queen of Coins
1. Eight of Coins
2. Eight of Staves
3. Ace of Swords, reversed
4. The Star
5. Two of Swords
6. The World, reversed
7. Three of Swords, reversed

Position 1

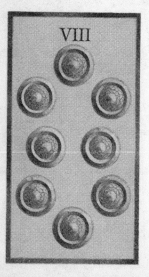

'The first card is the Eight of Coins which is truly amazing because it so often turns up when the Questioner is changing his or her job! This is a good omen because it tells me that the job is going to be better than your last one, but that you will have to work hard in order to justify the higher status that you are being given.'

Position 2

'Another astonishing card — this time you have drawn the Eight of Staves which is associated with travel. So even a complete beginner could work out that you are starting a new job which will involve some travelling around for you — let alone the fact that this particular job is actually in the travel trade.'

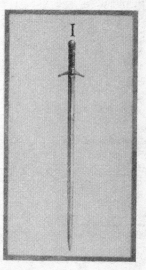

Position 3

'This is supposed to show past influences and it is the Ace of Swords which is reversed. I guess that there were some pointless arguments at your last job and complete failure to reach any kind of agreement.'

'Yes, that's right,' agreed Helen.

Position 4

'Here we have the future influence and you have picked just about the best card that you could because it is the Star. This card represents hope, optimism and faith in the future, so you should have plenty of good things to look forward to.'

Position 5

'This is supposed to be your direction or action for the future, and here you have the Two of Swords which is a strange card to choose for this position because it represents *inaction*. You are being advised to go along with whatever your new bosses want of you and not to

make any unnecessary waves and not to jump to conclusions. In short, just put the new job out on the water and see how it floats. Do you understand this?'

'Yes,' said Helen. 'I guess that it means I should just go along with their ideas and see how things work out.'

'Yes, that's right.'

Position 6

'This should throw some light on your future environment. The card shown here is the World which is a good card but it is actually reversed. This shows that you will not get everything that you are looking for but should, nevertheless, find your new world enlightening and interesting. You will have to watch out for something though. You may not be able to travel as much, at least in the initial stages, as you would like to. There is also another thought which crosses my mind here and that is that you should find yourself heading more towards an administrative role rather than purely that of travel clerk soon.'

Position 7

'This is supposed to represent the outcome and here you have drawn a difficult card. This is the Three of Swords, and it is reversed. I don't really know what to say to you about this. The reversed position should imply an end of sadness and worry. Is this trying to tell us that there

is going to be trouble from some unexpected source soon, I wonder? This is an inconclusive outcome so I suggest that we go around again for some clarification.'

'All right, I'll pick another seven, shall I?' asked Helen.

'Yes, go ahead and pick out some more.'

Second spread
Significator, Queen of Coins
1. Six of Swords, reversed
2. Death, reversed
3. Ten of Staves, reversed
4. Three of Staves, reversed
5. Six of Staves
6. The Moon, reversed
7. The Emperor

The second reading
'We'll keep the same significator here and start again, OK?'

Position 1

'Now we have the Six of Swords, reversed. Yes, it seems as if there will be some storms ahead as this card in the reversed position reminds me of a boat travelling into stormy water. It also tells me again that you could find yourself either travelling more or less than you suppose and that there will be practical problems associated with travel.'

Position 2
'This is the Death card and it is reversed. This shows that the change
of job is not going to be a complete change of life. If the card were
upright, you could expect to move house, change relationships or have
some other kind of complete change in your life. As it happens this
is going to change the way you work, the way you view work and
the way you view yourself in some way. You will find yourself losing
some old friends now and having to reassess those friendships which
you now have — that is another of the meanings attached to the Death
card when it is reversed.'

Position 3
'Here we have the Ten of Staves which is reversed. This is supposed
to represent the past and it shows that you have not yet had to take
much responsibility. As yet, you have no experience of taking decisions
or of being in charge of others. You will have to cope with this in the
near future.'

'That worries me a bit, I have to admit,' Helen said.

'Yes, I can see that it would.'

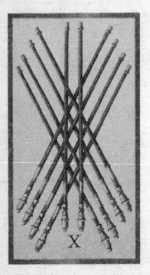

Position 4

'The future, and it is represented by the Three of Staves which is also reversed. This shows that there will be new projects for you but they might be difficult, delayed or even taken out of your hands somewhat. You will not be able to carry out your plans exactly as you would want, and you may have things shelved for you just when you think you are ready to go ahead.'

Position 5

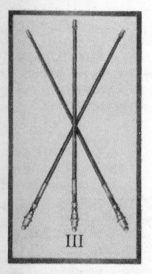 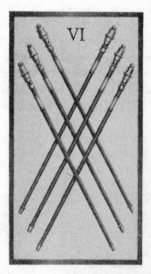

'This is your suggested future action and it is the Six of Staves. Well, this is a *very* good card as it means victory and achievement. This means that you will work to overcome your problems by negotiation because the Stave cards do indicate cooperation and negotiation on a sensible and non-emotional level. This is a very businesslike attitude which you will have to adopt.'

Position 6

'This shows the outside factors and the card is the Moon which is also reversed. In a way this is the worst card to find in this placement because it shows some uncertainty or lack of clarity in the environment around you. If the card were upright I would warn you not to trust the word of anyone around you, but the reversed Moon is not all that bad, it just shows that things may not be all they appear to be. You might be misled; there are factors which will gradually become clearer as time goes on. It also shows that some *emotional* factor outside of your control could affect you at second hand. If I had to give an example of what might happen, there could be a romance going on within the firm which could be embarrassing or awkward for you to witness. Frankly it is impossible to see at this stage where the trouble will come from but you must expect some and it will be woven around with some lies and misunderstanding. The source of this could be jealousy of your abilities or your success. This card also indicates fewer opportunities for travel than you had hoped for and it could also show that you might become involved with different parts of the world than you have formerly been involved with. Also, use your intuition; the reversed Moon shows great intuition on the part of the Questioner.'

Position 7
'This is the outcome, or in fact, the outcome of the outcome, if you see what I mean.'

'Yes, I do see.'

'The card is the Emperor and this shows categorically that this job, despite any setbacks and disappointments along the way, will put you firmly on the road to material success. That means that you can expect to earn good money, in time, and that you should be able to achieve the kind of position that you seek. You might end up running a branch for this firm (or another), or you might even in the long run be able to have your own business.'

'Owzat?'

'Sounds great, doesn't it?' enthused Helen.

'Yes, this should be a step along the road to success for you. Be happy, be confident, be prepared to work hard.'

After the reading

There wasn't much discussion after this reading as nearly all the events mentioned in it relate to the future. Helen told me that she had been unhappy in her last job, and that her first impressions of this new job seemed favourable. She said that they seemed to be expecting a lot of her and that she would have to be in charge of others for the first time, just as the cards predicted. She told me that there were a number of different departments within the firm and that there seemed to be rivalry and occasional friction between them. Helen felt that the reading would be most useful over the next few months as events began to reveal themselves.

The Consequences Spread with Major Arcana Only

I used only the Major cards in this spread, all in the upright positions. I also used a significator.

1. The person or situation.
2. Matters affecting the person or situation.
3. The past.
4. The future.
5. Suggested course of action.
6. Outside factors.
7. Consequence.

Linda

Linda is a very attractive lady in her mid-thirties — she has a striking Mediterranean type of appearance. She is living with her fiancé, Tony; a kindly man whose gentle, relaxed exterior hides an extremely acute mind which can sum up people and judge business situations in a flash. Until recently, Linda ran her own fashion business, but that has now been sold and she is temporarily out of work and wondering where she should go from here.

Significator, Queen of Coins
1. The Chariot
2. The Hermit
3. The Star
4. The Fool
5. The Hierophant
6. The Lovers
7. Judgement

The reading

QUEEN OF COINS

The significator
'I have chosen the Queen of Coins to represent you, Linda, partly due to your masses of black hair and also due to your business ability and practical turn of mind.'

Position 1
'In the centre of the spread we see the Chariot, which means that you are going to need to take into account a number of demands which are now being made upon you. You've got home needs, Tony's needs and your own requirements. You feel that you want to be back at work or at least busy, because the Chariot implies doing something with a purpose. This is occasionally connected with vehicles, so this could be an important part of your future in some way — you could be travelling soon. The Chariot is a quite unusual card in that it can sometimes be retroactive, and the observations which I have just made may have more to do with your past activities than with future events.'

Position 2
'Here we see the Hermit and this is really the situation which you are in now. You are at home on your own, thinking, going into yourself,

developing the thoughtful, spiritual side. Relaxing a bit, taking a holiday or a retreat from life. Perhaps, this is something that you need to do at this time.'

Position 3
'This is supposed to represent the past and it seems that you have achieved a lot in the past because you have the Star here at the back of you. You've been extremely creative in the past. You've made things work, made your life work, you've reached for the stars, learned a lot, studied a lot and gained a lot of insight and wisdom. You've kept a hopeful, optimistic and happy outlook on life.'

Position 4
'This position represents the events which are just ahead of you and now we see the Fool which is a fresh beginning. Nothing remains the same for long and you won't remain in this static position for long either. The Fool does mean something completely new: you will not be working in the same trade or the same way that you did before — you may find a completely different way of living. The ground is not going to be familiar. You seem to be setting off on a journey which

is much more of a spiritual journey than a physical one. You'll be busy again but not in the way you have been in the past.'

Position 5
This is the Hierophant which is, among other things, a card of marriage. This reading is taking place in February, I know that you are planning on getting married in July, so the fact that this is the fifth card in the spread and the number on the Hierophant card is also five seems to be significant as you intend being married five months from now. Interesting isn't it?

There is a feeling that you could be attached to Tony in more ways than marriage — you could be working together in some way. There is a jointness about this. This card is also about tradition and about doing things in a traditional way. You wouldn't be getting into anything crooked or dodgy; all your dealings will be straightforward and rather old-fashioned.'

Position 6
'Another nice card here, the Lovers. This card implies choice and this position represents the outside environment, therefore you will be

offered a certain number of choices from the outside. On another level, this shows that you intend doing things together and you will take decisions together. Whatever you do will involve teamwork, a group of people — you won't be on your own.'

Position 7

'The outcome of all this is shown here by the Judgement card. This is a card of reward and completion, therefore I feel that you will be pleased to be regularizing your relationship into a formal marriage and partnership. You seem to have run a complete circuit in your life and completed a phase. There will be a sense of reward and completion, a completely clean slate which allows you to move forward into a new phase with confidence.'

After the reading

We had quite a long chat after this reading, during which Linda told me that she was interested in doing some kind of spiritual work herself: she particularly felt that she wanted to become a healer. She also said that she had never been a 'mother earth' figure and now felt that she wanted to experience this through her marriage with Tony; Linda also told me that she would like to have a baby. (Linda has been married before but has no children.) She felt that she would be involved with Tony on a business level but had no plans to go back to work or back into business for herself at this time. She commented that they are short of money right now and I thought it very significant that she was not responding to this shortage by immediately finding work. Frankly, Linda wants to experience family life rather than business life now and, even more fortunately, Tony is in total agreement. I hope they can start a family soon and that their love will continue to grow — even if they are temporarily short of money.

The Celtic Cross

This spread is called after its shape, as a Celtic Cross has four arms of equal length. It is a very popular spread among amateur and professional Readers alike. It is best used to focus on a particular aspect of a Questioner's life but, even if it is used just to see what's there, it tends to pick out a particular question and focus itself on that. It gives a lot of insight into a problem as it shows the background to the situation and the environment surrounding it. Its drawback is that it is difficult for a beginner to use as there is probably a bit too much information to be absorbed at one time.

Timing events using the Celtic Cross
My friend, Jean Goodey, who is a professional Tarot Reader of great skill and understanding, passed on this idea to me some years ago and I have included it here as it can be so useful.

Firstly, lay out the Celtic Cross spread using both Arcanas of the Tarot. Then go *backwards* through the spread until you reach a number card (that is a card of the Minor Arcana which has a number from 1 to 10). Then work out your timing like this:

Years are indicated by a Coin card.
Months are indicated by a Sword card.
Weeks are indicated by a Stave card.
Days are indicated by a Cup card *but only if it is next to a Coin card!*

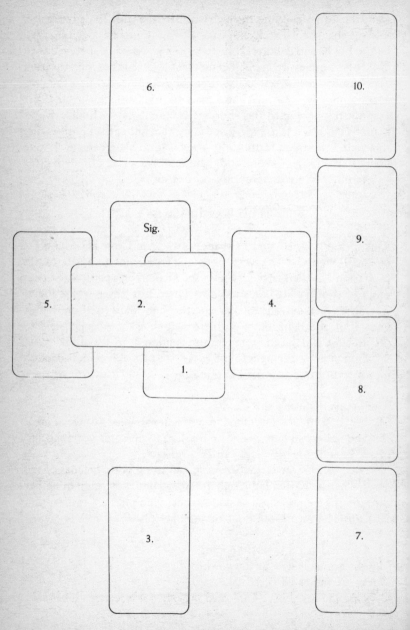

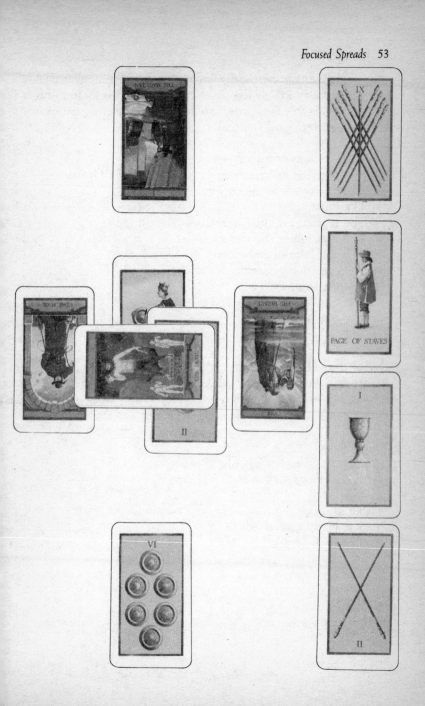

Jean tells me that she usually encounters her first numbered card among the four cards which are alongside the Cross itself. If this is not so, she says that the Reader should just keep on going backwards until a numbered card is found.

The Celtic Cross positions
1. The problem or circumstance surrounding the Questioner.
2. What he or she is up against.
3. The distant past.
4. The recent past, the present.
5. The near future.
6. The goal, aim or ambition of the Questioner.
7. The Questioner's feelings.
8. Outside factors.
9. The Questioner's hopes and fears.
10. The outcome.

Denise
Denise is small and thin with curly blonde hair. She reminds me of a sparrow as her actions and thinking patterns are very fast. She has the sense of humour and ready wit typical of her Gemini Sun sign. Denise made a few welcome comments here and there during the reading.

Significator, Queen of Swords
1. Two of Coins, reversed
2. The Devil
3. Six of Coins
4. The Hermit, reversed
5. The Fool, reversed
6. The Magician, reversed
7. Two of Staves, reversed
8. Ace of Cups
9. Page of Staves
10. Nine of Staves

QUEEN OF SWORDS

II

The reading
'First of all, I would like to choose a significator for you. This card
is supposed to represent you, yourself, in the reading. As you are a
quick-minded rather busy type of person, I think I will go for the Queen
of Swords.'

Position 1
'The card which is covering the significator is the Two of Coins,
reversed. Tell me Denise, are you about to be divorced?'
  'I was divorced last month,' Denise confirmed.
  'OK, I expect this reading will focus on events surrounding your
break up. You see the Two of Coins is supposed to represent coping
with life, juggling with money, making ends meet, which I'm sure is
an important problem for you at the moment, but it so often seems
to imply a division of resources, the kind of division which follows
a divorce.'

Position 2
'The second card, the one that crosses over the significator, is supposed
to show what you want from life or, perhaps, those things which are

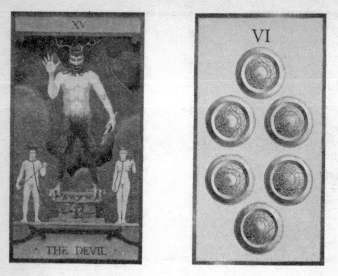

standing in the way of your progress and preventing you from achieving your aims. In this case the card is the Devil. This card represents commitment and responsibilities, often those associated with relationships, also sex. It can also mean enlightenment of an almost psychic nature. Let's progress with the reading and see why this should be such a big issue just now.'

Position 3
'This is supposed to represent the distant past and here you have the Six of Coins. Normally this could be considered a card of great benevolence, belonging to someone who has so much money coming in that they can afford to give it away. I feel, however, that in this case the card is saying that you have paid out both money and energy for your family in larger quantities than you could really afford, that you have paid your dues and now owe nothing to anybody either financially or morally.'

Position 4
'The recent past and present is shown by the Hermit which is reversed. The Hermit card shows that you are on your own, but, as it is reversed,

you may not be completely alone or may not be alone for long. You will have to withdraw a little from life now, rest your nerves and take some time to work out where you want to go from here. This card can also show that you haven't always been using common sense, that you have been going round and round in circles and behaving in an over-emotional manner, with justification of course, but nevertheless . . . There is another message here which is that you have spiritual or psychic abilities which have yet to be developed. The Hermit points to this and also the Devil card which can mean spiritual enlightenment in a reading.'

Denise stopped me and said, 'I discovered a couple of years ago that I am psychic and have recently been asked to join a development circle.'

'The cards seem to think that's a good idea, but take it slowly because the Hermit is reversed which shows that you might not be quite ready to *give* too much out to others just yet.'

'It's funny, Sasha, I've had two or three readings recently and they have all come up with this spiritual thing. I feel that I want to develop and direct the awareness which seems to be growing in me now.'

'Well,' I said, 'you've been through a divorce recently and that kind of struggle often seems to accelerate any tendency to psychic or spiritual abilities. Suffering seems to open one's inner eye in some way; it is a very well known phenomenon. Anyway, back to business.'

Position 5
'Here you have the Fool, reversed, and this shows that you are a bit hesitant and fearful about the future. You have to make a completely new start and you are naturally nervous about it. Also you don't want to make a fool of yourself again.'

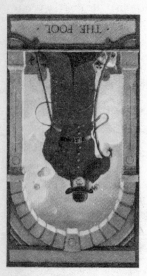 

Position 6
'This represents your goal, aims and ambitions, and the card which you have drawn here is an interesting one because it is the Magician, reversed. If it were upright it would show that you are ready to take charge of your life, take chances and start something big, but it is reversed and therefore it could show, for example, that you would not at the moment be interested in going into business for yourself. You would feel much safer being an employee rather than an employer. You must be careful in the future not to be tricked because the reversed Fool and Magician ahead of you seem to show that you could be defrauded or used in some sort of way and you need to be very careful

of this. You will have to take some slightly adventurous steps in the future but your hesitation could make you "miss the bus" so to speak.

Position 7

'This position is supposed to show how you affect the environment around you. This time we have the Two of Staves, reversed. I think this again is the partnership which you have recently emerged from and, as this is supposed to be *your* action which affects others around you, one could safely assume that it was *you* who left the marriage, no?'

'Yes,' confirmed Denise, 'I was the one to leave.'

'You might be uncertain about future relationships just now,' I added, 'and even have some difficulty with working relationships due to the fact that the cards are Staves.'

'Things are not too bad at the moment but there might be problems ahead, I suppose.'

Position 8

'This is the environmental factor and that's another odd one because that's the Ace of Cups. This shows that your future environment will be much more kind and loving that the one you've got now and that will only happen when you turn your back on the marriage and the past.'

Denise interrupted, 'I'm not really out of the past situation yet because the children are still living with him and I go there to see them. This causes a good deal of heartache all the way round.'

'I understand.'

Position 9

'This is supposed to represent your hopes, wishes and fears regarding the situation and this card is the Page of Staves. This has probably got something to do with the children and your longing for them to be OK. They should be all right anyway because the card is upright. This is also about friendship and being able to talk to people, about writing, travelling, communicating and working, so really I think you are hoping that all these things will help to make a better future for you.'

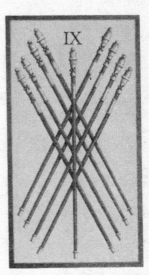

Position 10

'The last card represents the outcome and it is the Nine of Staves, which means level pegging really. You're on firm ground there, you are headed toward a certain amount of equilibrium. It seems as if you could be walking away completely from the marriage situation in a matter of weeks actually, finding a way of seeing the children and dealing with the ex-husband in a way which works. The Staves are supposed to represent weeks, so we can take this to be nine weeks if you like — that's how long it will take to sort out finally.'

After the reading
'Because the Magician is in the goal position but reversed, I feel that you are not really clear about your own goal. You are still coming out of the divorce situation and the aftermath, and have no real idea of where you should be headed now.'

Denise nodded, 'I have lots of options and I'm not really clear about the future myself yet. I'm not sure which way I want to go.'

'Yes, your first problem is to sort out yourself, your routine of seeing the children away from the ex-marital home, and resting from the over-activity of the past year. You see, Denise, if the Magician were the right way up, it would indicate major projects, but this reversal shows a *hesitant* step forward without too much risk attached. It does involve using skills — salesmanship for instance — therefore you can go forward slowly.'

'Funny that you mention salesmanship,' commented Denise, 'because I do actually work in sales as I'm a representative for an engineering company.'

'That fits in well, doesn't it? This could imply that your firm will not be doing too well in the future. You know, there could be some doubts about this job. You might have to think eventually about finding another.

'I also feel quite strongly that your husband may be putting on some kind of an act and that any bad behaviour on his part is purely designed to wind you up. I think you might have some kind of revelation about him which will surprise you, because the Devil is often indicative of enlightenment. Does this make sense to you?'

'Yes, it does,' said Denise. 'You see, my children are in their teens now and more or less off my hands. They have stayed with my ex-husband because they are finishing courses at schools nearby, although they do come down to me during the holidays. All the time that I keep going back into that house, my ex, just as you have said, winds me up and makes me feel guilty, but I know in my heart that I have done the right thing. I couldn't take his violence and bullying any longer.

'The children are seeing him in his true colours for the first time now, as they are now on the receiving end of his moods. All at once, I'm no longer just neurotic old Mum, so there is a measure of enlightenment there too. My job is secure but the firm, as you said, is not doing all that well. I could change jobs in the future if it became necessary.

'The reading,' said Denise, thoughtfully, 'to be fair, has told me things that I was already aware of, but it has made me face up to one or two things that I didn't want to look at too closely such as making a fool of myself emotionally due to vulnerability, and also the view that my ex-husband is not as put out as he is trying to make out.'

The Celtic Cross with Major Arcana

There are many people who produce perfectly good readings with only Major Arcana cards. Some Readers use the Major Arcana cards from one deck in order to give an introductory reading, then give a fuller reading with a complete deck. Personally, I find the Major Arcana alone difficult to read: I prefer to 'back up' the Major cards with a couple of Minor ones.

The Celtic Cross lends itself to a Major Arcana reading because it requires only ten cards and, as there are only twenty-two Major cards to choose from, this seems a sensible way to demonstrate them at work on their own.

The Celtic Cross is probably the most frequently used spread, at least in Britain. It is described in practically every book on the Tarot and seems to be the first one that everyone learns. However, I think this is a difficult spread for a beginner to deal with and I often suggest that it is left until the student is a bit more experienced. Many people use it to give a 'blanket' reading, just to see what comes up. That idea will work well if you give the reading for someone whom you know well, because you know something of that person's circumstances and can link in to the particular aspect of their life which appears to be accented by the cards. It is not so easy to do this for a total stranger, and this leads to a certain amount of 'fishing' in order to find the

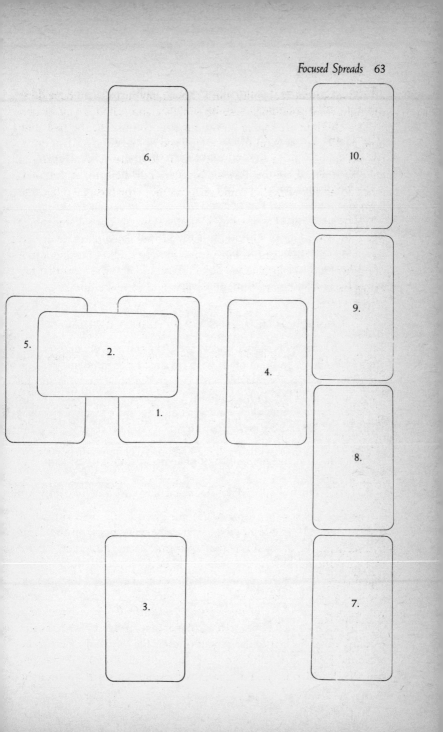

particular problem or area of interest. It is, however, well suited to concentrating on one specific situation.

The Celtic Cross with Major Arcana — positions
1. The problem or circumstance surrounding the Questioner.
2. What he or she is up against.
3. The distant past.
4. The recent past, the present.
5. The near future.
6. The goal, aim or ambition of the Questioner.
7. The Questioner's feelings.
8. Outside factors.
9. The Questioner's hopes and fears.
10. The outcome.

Mike
Mike is an attractive man with wavy grey hair and a lovely mischievous smile. He seems to be content with his life at the moment. He tells me that he is happily married with two grown children who are still living at home. He is in business with a partner and both he and the partner can see a time in the somewhat distant future when they might want to sell up the business, part company and do something more restful. As Mike didn't appear to have any pressing problems, we decided to take a look at the possibility of changes in the business aspect of his life, as and when it occurs.

As I was using only the Major Arcana, I didn't use a significator with this spread.

No significator.
1. The Hierophant
2. Death
3. Judgement, reversed
4. Wheel of Fortune, reversed
5. The Fool, reversed
6. The Emperor
7. The Sun, reversed
8. The High Priestess, reversed

   9. **The Lovers, reversed**
10. **The Devil**

The reading

Position 1

'The first card is the Hierophant. This card has a religious look about it but its symbolic meaning is much nearer to the idea of *tradition*. It shows me that your life is stable, similar to the lives of other people who are around you, and that it has been running along the same lines for some time. You are a traditional type of family man with old-fashioned values of honesty and decency which spill over into your business dealings. It seems that we have quite a strange situation here. I deliberately didn't select a significator to represent you due to the fact that we are using only Major Arcana cards; however, it seems as if we have been given a significator for you whether we like it or not!'

Position 2

'The second card is the Death card which shows that the life you are living now will *not* go on in the same way indefinitely. Something will have to come to a complete end so that a new beginning can occur. The Death card does not mean that *you* are about to die, just that the matter under examination, i.e. your future business situation, is going to come to an end, therefore clearing the way for something new. The picture of a skeleton on this card shows me that you will have to think something through very thoroughly soon; strip it down to the bare bones, so to speak.'

Position 3
The third position shows the distant past; here you have the Judgement card and it is reversed. The picture on the card is of Gabriel blowing his horn on Resurrection Day and, because the card is reversed, there

has been some event or situation in the past which you don't want to see resurrecting itself and occurring again. As this reading is specifically related to business matters, this indicates poor judgement in the past, decisions and choices which did not work out well, and possibly even legal troubles related to business. You have suffered losses at some past date and obviously don't wish to do so again. You are not a gambler by nature, the Hierophant tells me that. There is no reason to *assume* that bad judgement and losses will happen again in the future, but it is obviously something that you fear as it still lingers in your memory or it wouldn't have shown up in the reading.'

Position 4

'This represents the present and the recent past, and the card is the Wheel of Fortune which, in this case, is reversed. I don't see the Wheel as being too bad, but it tells me that circumstances regarding your work at present are not all that easy. All businesses have been through a recession and you may be feeling tired from all the effort which it requires. My feeling here is that the Wheel is still turning, somewhere just out of sight, which leads me to believe that there are things going on in other heads — your partner's most probably — which could have a profound effect on your life in the future.'

 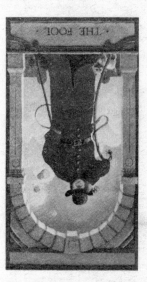

Position 5

'This position is supposed to represent your immediate future influence. The card is the Fool and it is reversed. The card is symbolic of new beginnings; the Fool is not foolish, just lacking in experience. He is setting out on a new path, taking an unfamiliar route and, therefore, lacks the wisdom of experience. If we apply the card to your career it shows me that you fear change and would prefer to stay in your present situation even though it seems to be tiresome, rather than go out on a limb and try something completely new. This card in the reversed position sometimes shows a kind of mental paralysis: even though you will be shown opportunities, you will doubt your ability to grasp them and to make them work. Ultimately, I feel you will be compelled to make a complete change due to the fact that the Death card is lying across the self-selected significator.'

Position 6

'This position is supposed to show your goal, or the direction you are or should be aiming for. The card here is the Emperor which strongly emphazises material achievement. It can represent the employer in the case of one who is employed, or the Questioner himself if he runs his own business. It shows that your goal is to be your own boss, run your own business and to achieve material success, security and independence.'

Position 7

'This is supposed to be how you see your environment either now or in the future. Here you have the Sun card and it is reversed. This card is a good card either way up, but the beneficial aspects of the card are slightly weakened when it is reversed. If it were the right way up, you would have a very optimistic outlook on the future — even with the reversal, you can be reasonably optimistic but there is a blending of caution here too. It's a card which to me represents the growing of crops and the harvest; in your case, you have gained a good deal from your past efforts but perhaps not as much as you would like. I find that this card often has something to do with children and this shows me that you may worry about your children. You could hope that your son would take over your business or join you in some way, but this reversed card seems to militate against that happening. My tricky mind tells me that you may worry about your partner's children and his intentions regarding them and the future of the business.'

Position 8

'The next card is an odd one because it is the Priestess which is also reversed, and it is in the position which refers to environmental factors. This could mean that, if you are going to go into a new environment, you would need to find out all you could about it. If you sell up your present business and go into something smaller, easier, you would need to make damned sure that you knew exactly what was what before diving in. The Fool there ahead of you shows the possibility of making a mistake. The Priestess also suggests that a formal course of study might be necessary. You could have difficulty with women around you; you might find that your wife and/or daughter need to be put clearly into the picture and not just faced with a *fait accompli'*.

Position 9
'Inner emotions, hopes and fears — here we have the Lovers, reversed. This shows me quite clearly that you wouldn't want to go into a partnership again with someone else, because the Lovers card so often implies partnership matters. I feel strongly that even though you have plenty of moral support from the family (the Hierophant would suggest that), you would not actively work in close conjunction with any of them. It does not look as if your son will come into the business, nor, for that matter, would your wife or daughter.'

Position 10

'Here we see the Devil. I don't necessarily see this as a bad card at all. It involves commitment, hanging on to things, or tying yourself down to some kind of responsibility. I think it is saying that whatever you decide to do eventually, you should look into all the practicalities before committing yourself. You will be in charge of your own business, the Emperor tells us that, so you will probably choose to bind yourself to something new.

'There is another way of looking at a part of this reading. The Lovers card tells me that you are not completely happy with your present partnership. Also that decisions which should be made jointly are being taken both by your partner and yourself without consultations. The Lovers card indicates joint decisions and all kinds of partnership matters. Your present partner may want to keep the business by passing his share on to *his* children (remember the Sun reversed). There is a possibility that he could try to tie you (the Devil) to an arrangement which means that this business continues with *you* working for the benefit of *his* children.

Postscript

Events have occurred since this reading which have borne out the problems which were foreseen. Mike has asked me not to go into details at this time but he wanted to report that the reading worked.

CHAPTER FIVE

Focused Spreads Which Allow One to Choose Between Two Roads

The Question and Answer Spread

This spread has been developed from an idea which was given to me by James Haslam. It asks you to concentrate on a specific question and then shows two possible paths of action. In this case the Questioner told me that he was not settled in his present job and wanted to know whether he should elect to stay there or look for something else. I explained to him that neither the cards nor I were really the best judge of the matter, and that in the last resort it would be up to him to make his own decision. However, we laid the cards out just to see if there was any clear indication.

On this occasion I asked the Questioner to shuffle the cards and then to spread the cards out face downwards on the table and to select two to represent the question. Then to select two groups of four cards — these were all still face downwards on the table. I then asked him to choose which group of four was to represent 'do I stay put and do nothing?' and which group was to represent 'shall I look for something else?' We then read the answer contained in each of the groups.

Group one

1.
2.
3.   } Answer one
4.

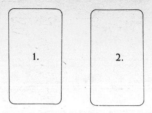

The question

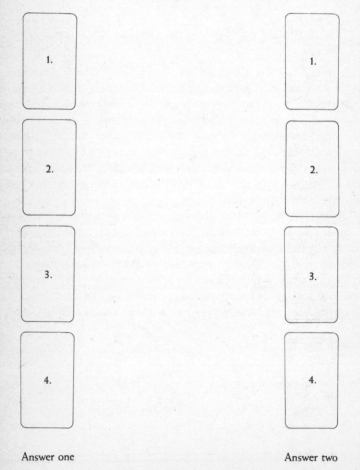

Answer one

Answer two

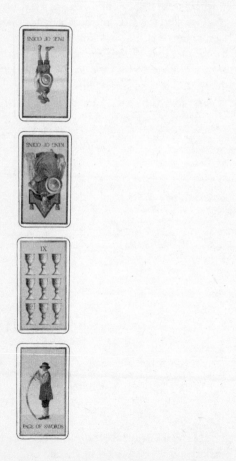

Group two

1.
2.
3.   } Answer two
4.

Ray

Ray is a lovely, cuddly man who would be any child's idea of a favourite uncle. He told me that he had worked for the same company for many years but that they had been taken over recently and he was worried about his position within the new regime. He felt, probably psychically, that he would have to make a change some time in the future. He wanted to know whether he should leave now and find something else or sit it out for a while at least and see how things worked out.

The question
1. Three of Swords, reversed
2. The Tower

Answer one — 'do I stay and do nothing?'
1. Page of Coins, reversed
2. King of Coins, reversed
3. Nine of Cups
4. Page of Swords

Answer two — 'do I go and look for another job?'
1. The Hierophant, reversed
2. The Moon
3. Strength, reversed
4. Ace of Cups, reversed

The reading

The question
'The two cards which represent the question are the Three of Swords, reversed and the Tower. Well, the Tower is a great shock and upheaval and that is what is going on in your working life right now. If the Three

of Swords were the right way up, there would be considerable loss and sadness, even health problems, but reversed it shows an unfortunate situation, a touch of regret at changes which are being forced on you. Also the Swords have got a slightly legal side to them as well.'

Answer one
'When we look at the "do I stay" cards, we have two Coin Court cards which are reversed and these, to my mind, represent either a person who is not entirely on your side or a kind of company policy, probably to do with money and efficiency, which is not going to suit you. If this shows an actual person who will cause difficulties, I feel that he would be a well-built man, with dark or greying hair and dark eyes.

'Satisfaction is very much at the core of your question here because we have the Nine of Cups which shows that you could, given a fair crack of the whip, make a satisfying job out of this if you stay put. At the end of this we have the Page of Swords which could show that you have someone spying on your behalf, there could be prior knowledge of some kind and there could also be a contract on the way to you. The point is that you have got a contract of employment

and your job is secure. It seems that you will find things difficult, but there is nothing here to suggest that you should leave immediately.'

Answer two
'Let us look at the "do I go" situation. Here we have the Hierophant which is reversed and that is telling me that if you were to leave now,

you would completely screw up everything you have ever worked for. You would be *seen* as being unreliable by a new boss. They would assume that you had flounced out just because the conditions changed.

'The Moon here means that any decision to move now would be made on an over-emotional basis and would be clearly concerned with wanting to leave something behind rather than being a considered decision to go *towards* something which you specially want. You would find yourself in a stop-gap job perhaps. You need to take some time to see clearly how your situation is going to turn out before you look realistically around for something new. The Moon represents illusion.

'The Strength card reversed shows that, if you *do* move now, either you will find your new job too heavy in some way or you will find yourself in a weak position in the new place; weaker than you are now. Also the Ace of Cups which is reversed on the end there shows that even the satisfaction which you have got now would be thrown away, it would go down the drain.'

Conclusion

'I think the answer is quite clear: even if the first pathway is not wonderful, it is tolerable, while the second one is truly awful. At least by staying you will have the satisfaction (Nine of Cups) of getting the right legal document, or contract (Page of Swords) which would give you fair treatment. The only upright card in the second pathway is the Moon, and this is usually a difficult card as it is associated with illusion, deception, moonlight and shifting sands. The Hierophant, which represents stability and tradition, is reversed here which shows that it would be nigh on impossible to find a stable and settled worthwhile job elsewhere just at the moment.'

After the reading

Ray told me that the problem was that his firm had recently merged with another larger company, and his job was due to be rationalized in such a way that he would have one rather boring routine ahead of him instead of the variety of chores which he has enjoyed up to now. He wondered if he could tolerate this situation. He took my point that a move should be a considered action rather than just leaving and hoping for better things to come. Considering the advice of the cards, he thought that he could either adjust his present job in some way or, at worst, look around at leisure for something else to take over when the period of his present contract came to an end.

The Two Pathways Spread

This very simple idea was given to me by Roy Sinclair. It utilizes the familiar shape of the seven-card Consequences spread in order to take a quick look at two pathways.

In this spread I used a significator and both Major and Minor Arcana cards, but all in the upright position.

1. The situation immediately confronting the Questioner.
2. Circumstances and feelings surrounding him.
3 & 5. Pathway one.
4 & 6. Pathway two.
7. The outcome.

Stuart

Stuart is a lively seventeen-year-old who is currently at college taking a course in computer and business studies. He sees this as a road to future security and self-respect at a time when so many young people have little chance of any kind of a job. What he would really like to do, however, is to work in the world of pop music. He plays the guitar and the piano, writes lyrics and music, and has played with other youngsters in a variety of casual groups. He is hoping that, in this day of computerized music, his computer skills will enable him to work on the programming side of the business.

Significator, The Magician
1. King of Staves
2. The Empress
3. Eight of Swords
4. The Sun
5. The Chariot
6. Judgement
7. The World

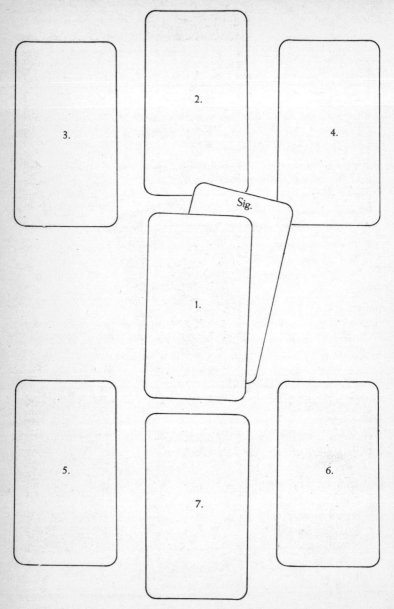

The reading

After taking a look at the cards, Stuart decided that he fancied the Magician as a significator. It is fairly unusual for someone to use a Major Arcana card as a significator, but there is nothing wrong in doing so.

Position 1

'Here we have the King of Staves and this seems to represent your view of the future, Stuart. I feel that you are aiming for the world of commerce and communications, whether in music or in something different.'

Position 2

'The Empress here shows that you have a terrific creative urge; you want to bring something of your own invention into being. You would be most unhappy to work as a cypher in some huge accounts company, for instance.'

Stuart commented that this was very true.

Positions 3 & 5

'You have chosen this route to represent your potential career in music.

The cards placed here are the Eight of Swords and the Chariot. The Eight seems to show that you shouldn't tie yourself down to a musical career which might not fit you for anything else later. There could be substantial difficulties in finding your way into this kind of work. It seems that you will have to keep your options open for a while. The Chariot shows that you *can* break into the music scene if you try hard enough, but the two horses on the card show me that you may have to do this in conjunction with other work. You will travel in connection with music and will come into contact with all kinds of people.'

Positions 4 & 6
'Now we will look at the prospect of a conventional career in business and computers. The Sun card here clearly shows that you will be able not only to work in this field but also to enjoy it and to be creative within its limitations. The Judgement card shows that you will be well rewarded for your work, also that you will pass your college exams while on the road to your career. However, there is something which, although apparently dead, will not lie down, therefore your long-held desire to work in music will resurrect itself later on.'

Position 7
'This is the outcome and here you have the World card. Frankly, Stuart,

the world is in your hands. You will succeed whatever you do, but the variety of elements encompassed by this card show that you will have experience of many fields of endeavour — creative, financial and mathematical. Yes, you will have some musical experience, but whether this comes first or is taken up later on, I really cannot say. One thing I can tell you is that you will be successful in whatever you do and that you will have a very full and interesting life.'

CHAPTER SIX

Focusing on One's Inner and Outer Feelings

The Jung Spread

I came across this spread many years ago and have used it on occasion ever since. It is the best way I know of identifying a matter of inner conflict. It seems that the fates led me to Dave, who turned out to be an excellent example of someone who is living and acting in one way in his day-to-day life while wanting to be and do something completely different. I had no way of knowing that Dave had this problem until after I had done the reading.

The Jung Spread positions
1.   The Questioner.
2 & 3. The anima. The way that the Questioner has been taught to think and behave, or what he has been programmed to believe is important.
4 & 5. The animus. How the Questioner acts in his day-to-day life in the light of this upbringing or mental programming.
6 & 7. The child. What he really wants and needs out of life.

Dave
Dave is a lovely, sincere, kind-hearted man who works for a large business firm. His smashing wife Jan works with animals and, despite being terribly short of money, admits to being totally contented. They have a lovely little girl called Helen and there is another baby on the way. Dave and Jan are both tall and Helen looks as if she is going to be tall, straight and friendly, just like her parents.

I asked Dave to shuffle the cards and then to hand me seven cards

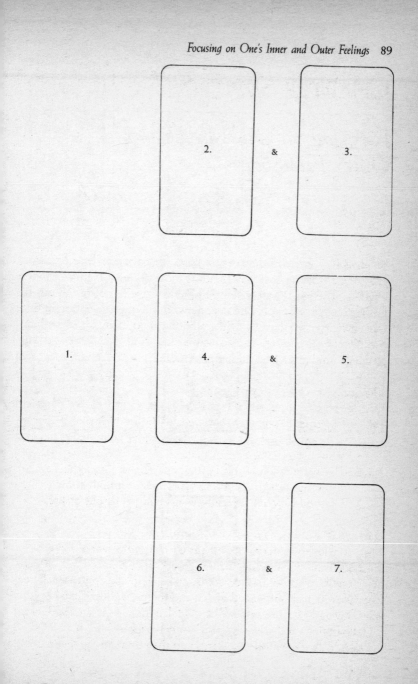

2.   &   3.

1.   4.   &   5.

6.   &   7.

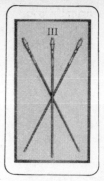

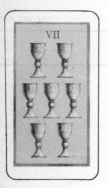

from the top, one card at a time. I then laid them out and turned them over in the required order. I used all the cards in the upright position for this spread; I did not use a significator.

1.   Seven of Cups
2 & 3. Death & Three of Staves
4 & 5. Six of Cups & Five of Swords
6 & 7. Queen of Coins & King of Swords

The reading

Position 1
'This is supposed to represent you yourself as you are right now. The Seven of Cups here, Dave, shows that you have got a number of options open at the moment and these could refer to home life, work or anything. You are looking at a variety of paths which could be right, and you may not know which one to choose, or you may have trouble working out what it is that you really want out of life. This card in itself shows some dissatisfaction with your inner sense of self-worth.'

Positions 2 & 3: The anima

'This position indicates what you think you *should feel*, what you think you *should want* and how you think you *should act*. The cards here are Death and the Three of Staves which show me that you have been trained to be very decisive and, therefore, you feel that you should be looking forward with relish to all the new projects which are ahead of you. You are telling yourself that you *should* feel confident and excited at the thought of putting your ideas into action in the near future.

 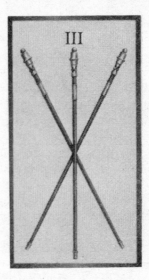

You are being required here to give an appearance of strength and machismo. You are being told that there are new projects — I know that you will be moving house shortly for instance — and you *should* be feeling absolutely delighted to be in such an active and upwardly mobile atmosphere.'

Positions 4 & 5: The animus

'The way that you are actually behaving is symbolized by these two cards which are the Six of Cups and the Five of Swords. This is a bit of a mixture really because the Six of Cups is a reminiscence card, a card of the past. Therefore you are still trying to behave in the manner

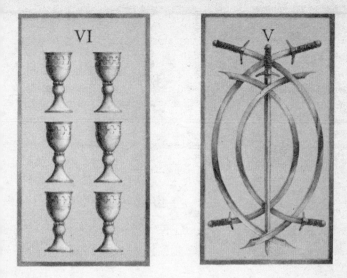

in which your parents brought you up and are still trying to fulfil their dreams. However, the Five of Swords is a card of extreme conflict and this can be found within yourself just now. You are discovering that you are not a clone of your parents, neither should you try to be the fulfilment of their dreams. You are yourself, and this realization is the cause of the current conflict within you because you are still trying to live in the past while also trying to find out who *you* are and what *you* need out of life. You could in some twisted sort of way feel slightly apologetic to your parents because you are now discovering that you are an individual and that you have different aspirations for yourself and your family than they had for you.'

Positions 6 & 7: *The child*

'This represents the reality of your inner desires. It seems that you feel the need to be both sociable and successful, but in a way which includes both intellect and profit. You need people and you want to be needed. The first card, which is the Queen of Coins, shows me that you are a very homeloving person, very practical, very down to earth. You need security, both financial and emotional, but the King of Swords

QUEEN OF COINS

KING OF SWORDS

is a pretty powerful card which shows the need to be the master of your own destiny and to work in the realm of ideas, theory and philosophy. This is because this card has connections with the element of 'air', or pure intellect. You seem inwardly to want professional status and to be known for some kind of mentally and physically creative endeavour. There is a need for independence, possibly independence of thought. You seem to want to be among people, to help them, and to interest them, rather than to aspire for success in business.'

The postscript — Dave's comments

'I felt that my parents decided everything for me,' said Dave, 'and that I didn't know for sure who I was or where I wanted to go.'

'Dave, I feel that you are a tremendously creative man, but that you don't know how to direct this creative urge.'

'I come from an artistic family,' Dave agreed, 'but I seem to have no particular artistic flair.'

'You seem to need a creative outlet,' I went on, 'not necessarily to impress people but in order to leave something of a mark on the world. You also want to help people; coupled with this I have a strong feeling that you are extremely psychic.'

'It's funny that you should mention that,' said Dave, 'because I find that people who've got problems often seem to come to me to talk them over, and I can often feel what is going on around them.'

'Dave, I have met quite a few people like you over the years; people who have definite psychic gifts but who don't have the training, therefore don't have the confidence to develop their skills. I cannot do anything about your apparent lack of artistic ability, except to tell you to keep trying all avenues until you find something which you can create. However, I can advise you to find the local Spiritualist church address in the 'phone book and to find a development circle, also to read books on Tarot, astrology, mediumship and psychic development in order to find out which of these, if any, you feel drawn towards. You are a psychic with a strong need to express this side of yourself, to find the power which is locked up in the King of Swords in a practical way as shown by the Queen of Coins. Does that help you?'

'Yes, Sasha,' Dave nodded, 'it has made me face up to the fact that I must do something both to develop psychically and creatively rather than just get on with my job and life in the ordinary day-to-day way.'

CHAPTER SEVEN

The String Section

String Readings with Various Interpretations

Whilst collecting material for this book, I began to realize that beginners find real difficulty in interpreting a group of cards when they are put together. They can sort out the meaning of individual cards, but cannot manage to apply them to a person's life. In this section I have experimented by stringing a few cards together in no particular spread and asking other readers to interpret them. The first attempt at this was really amusing. I collared some of the members of the committee of the British Astrological and Psychic Society and we chose one person to act as Questioner while several of us interpreted the cards which were selected.

The professionals

Renee agreed to act as guinea-pig because she doesn't read the cards herself: Renee is a medium, clairvoyant and rune reader. Our six Readers were Eve Bingham, who is a Tarot Reader, medium and clairvoyant; David Bingham who reads sand, crystal and anything else that is going, including Tarot; Gordon Smith, a medium, clairvoyant and Psy-card reader who also understands Tarot; Janis Huntley, an astrologer who also reads Tarot; and Fred Curtis, a numerologist who understands Tarot with a numerological emphasis. Well, if that lot couldn't read a string of Tarot cards, who in the world could?

Renee

First of all I will give you some background to the reading. Renee is a tall slim lady who looks far more like the brilliant statistician that she is than anyone's idea of a medium. She uses her mathematical talents by working in a large organization but she has been involved with clairvoyant work for many years now. Renee is a widow with two grown-up children who are themselves unmarried. The children live independent lives but often pop in to chat with Renee and are still very close to her. She also makes wonderful cakes.

Renee shuffled the cards, placed them face downwards on the table and picked out six at random. These were the six cards which she selected:

1. Page of Cups
2. Page of Swords
3. Knight of Cups
4. Page of Staves
5. Eight of Staves
6. Nine of Staves

Dave Bingham was the first to comment, telling us that she had picked a dreadful bunch of cards and asking if she could choose another group. I told him that he was a coward and that a Reader of his age and experience should be able to read anything. Dave then suggested that Eve start the interpretation.

While I furiously scribbled on a notepad Eve started her reading.

Eve's interpretation
'I can see the children here, still close to you this year. The Page of Cups would indicate that you yourself are female Renee.'

'I'm glad you told me that,' said Renee drily.

'You seem to be rather indecisive about going on a holiday this year, Renee.'

PAGE OF CUPS

PAGE OF SWORDS

VIII

KNIGHT OF CUPS

'That's true,' she agreed. 'I would love to go away but I have too many other commitments at the moment.'

'Well, Renee, I'm sure you *will* go away somewhere this year, that is shown by the Eight of Staves here and also by the Knight of Cups. Knights do indicate movement and I see this one as showing overseas travel. There seems to be some kind of hesitation though — you will find it hard to make up your mind. Despite the fact that you are over-committed financially just now and very busy, I'm sure you will get away and that it will be important in some way.'

You will notice that Eve did *not* read the cards in strict rotation but mentally rearranged them into groups which represented connected ideas. The other readers also grouped the cards into connected ideas — Fred Curtis's reading is another good example. This is *Tarot in Action*.

Dave's reading

'This layout is terrible, there's no guts to it, no problems to get your teeth into.'

Eve glanced at him impatiently, 'Get on with it, Dave!'

'Well, I can see that Renee will have things to sort out this year but there is nothing she cannot handle. The Pages of Cups and Swords could certainly mean her children, but there seem to be new emotional beginnings as shown by the Knight of Cups. Renee, you're definitely

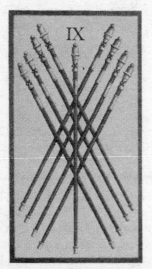

PAGE OF STAVES

going away and I would say you will travel in the late summer or early autumn.'

'How do you get the timing on this, Dave?' I asked.

'Well the Eight of Staves, could be August, the eighth month, the Nine of Staves could also apply to September. There does seem to be a change at work following this holiday; perhaps a complete change of direction. This would be shown by the Page of Staves which is often related to news plus the Nine of Staves which shows you being in command of a situation but at the same time hemmed in, not free to move. The other cards, the Eight and the Knight show freedom — or at least the need for freedom — so the structure of your job could be changing in some way. Of course, you *could* meet an influential foreigner while you are away.'

Gordon's suggestions
'Yes, I also felt it was something about work. There seems to be a reasonably happy situation both before and after the changes. I'm sure you will have to face changes after you come back from your travels, but there's no doubt that it can be sorted out.'

Janis's suggestions
'The Nine seems to show structure and organization which will materialize from a completely new venture. However the Page of Staves which follows the Knight of Cups seems to show feelings of confusion, a feeling of "have I done the right thing?"'

Fred's suggestions
'The Pages seem to show that you are young at heart at the moment and would probably welcome a new venture now. There is definitely movement forward shown by the Knight of Cups; it seems to be in the right direction. There is skill shown in the Page of Swords but with support behind as shown by the Nine of Staves. There could be new ideas (Swords) of a creative nature (Staves) but also emotionally pleasing (Cups).'

Dave agreed that this could well be creative and fulfilling.

Eve suggested that the Nine of Staves shows that most of Renee's obstacles are behind her now.

My feelings about the spread

I felt that her children were still going to be a close influence on Renee's life. She would travel, probably to a watery place, Eight of Staves being travel and the Knight of Cups being associated with water. Douglas Ashby, another member of our merry band, considers the Pages to be single people, and it is worth noting that Renee and her children are all unmarried.

Renee's job could change in some way and that could start in the form of some document or even a form of contract (Page of Swords). Eve said that she considered the Page of Swords to suggest indecision. This difference of opinion was, in fact, the only one which we had. Amazingly, all six of us saw the reading in much the same way. We all felt that she would start something new and creative with possibly young people around. We all hoped that the Knight of Cups would turn out to be a lover for Renee — Renee said that she hoped so too!

As you can see this was all tremendous fun, but it did show how even such a diabolical layout as the one Renee picked could be turned into quite an interesting story. We will all have to wait until the end of this year to see how it works out.

Postscript

This reading has not come true at all! Perhaps the cards have taken us too far into the future by showing us events which will occur next year or the year after. That's Tarot for you!

Dave Bingham and I collaborated on another string reading. This time we used Victoria as our guinea pig. The cards were easier to read and the reading was rather more serious, but the idea was the same: just six cards in no special layout with no particular meanings allotted to the position of any of the cards.

Victoria

Dave knows Victoria better than I do — I wasn't sure, for instance, whether she has a husband. She is a neatly dressed, dark-haired woman whose rather tough and worldly exterior hides a very soft and sensitive heart. She is a skilful palmist who has a wide knowledge of her craft. She is very attached to her family and friends and gets a lot of pleasure out of her work. She loves to travel whenever she can afford to do so.

A Second String

These were the six cards which Victoria selected:

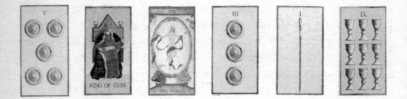

1. Five of Coins
2. King of Cups
3. The World
4. Three of Coins
5. Ace of Staves
6. Nine of Cups

Dave's reading

'You seem to feel down-hearted just now — this is shown by the Five of Coins. You could also be very worried about money matters.'

'That's true,' said Victoria.

'I think the second card, the King of Cups, could be your husband and it seems as if he is very happy with the way things are going. He sees your work as bringing him into a new world, this being shown by the World card which is next to him. The Three of Coins on the other side of the World shows a comfortable home on the one hand, and a good structure or basis to his life on the other. This does not seem to take into account your feelings: I think there is too much

satisfaction in him, too much taking for granted.

'The next card is the Ace of Staves and this seems to show the way that I think you see yourself going over the next year or two. The Ace

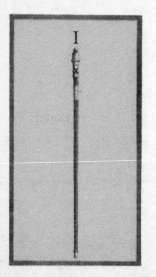

of Staves is a card of birth, or of re-birth, and this shows that you are hoping that the successes which you are beginning to have now, the money which you should be able to earn soon, will give you the freedom to be yourself.

'The last card is the Nine of Cups and this is what you are definitely looking for because it shows great personal satisfaction. You're not going to let him take it all away from you. There is a feeling that you will soon emerge as a winner and will go hard and fast for what you want — probably for the first time in your life.'

My feelings about this reading

'Victoria, you seem to feel as if you are out in the cold in some way now. There is a man as shown by the King of Cups but he is either not helping you just now, or hasn't yet appeared in your life. The Five of Coins is a strange card. It usually concerns money losses, but it is such a lonely card; it is as if one knows that love and understanding exist somewhere indoors but that one cannot find the door to the house. There seems to be no way to get through to him and show him how you feel. If the King of Cups turns out to be a man you have yet

KING OF CUPS

to meet, then things will obviously change — for the better, I hope.

'Something *is* going to change fairly soon: your world will be different, and this is suggested by the World card just here. There could be travel, new faces and places, a new meaning to life. It seems as if there will be a feeling of completion soon. This is not the harsh kind of ending that a card like the Death card would bring but a kind of rounding off, a feeling of having done your job and finished it for good.

'The Three of Coins could indicate a new house or business premises. On another level, it shows a job well done but more challenges ahead. There is a rather peculiar and very old-fashioned meaning to this card, which has been handed down from the time when a craftsman or trader could receive patronage from the local aristocrat. Even if the craftsman never saw any payment for the job, it gave his company the kind of cachet which lured other more lucrative work his way. In these days it would be some other rich and powerful force — the media, for example.

'The Ace of Staves is a new start and a creative one at that. There will be arrangements to be made, business matters to settle, but they will be very good. The last card suggests a satisfactory outcome, with

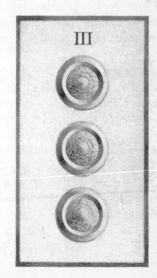

or without a man in your life. This is shown by the Nine of Cups.
You will have personal satisfaction but this may not be extended to
everyone else around you. This time *they* could be the ones to be left
out in the cold, and it could be a novel experience for them.'

After the reading
Victoria told me that she was, as Dave had known, married with grown-
up children. Her husband was quite difficult to live with and she was
now attempting to put herself in a position where she would no longer
feel beholden to him for money. She also wanted some kind of creative
outlet of her own and now seemed to be finding it. This too would
ultimately lead to feelings of independence. She hoped that the reading
would work out accurately, but wasn't so sure that she wanted another
man in her life — just in case the King of Cups did not turn out to
be Robert, her husband.

A few hints

If you take a small number of cards you are more likely to be able to pick out some kind of theme than to succeed in making up a story from a welter of cards laying on the table. When you begin to find this kind of reading easy, then try to apply the cards, making positions for home, work, health, travel, etc., placing two or three cards on each position. There are some old Romany ideas which, in a modernized form, make good material for simple exercises. Here are one or two of them.

Take a few cards and give them the following designations:
1. The past.
2. The Questioner's feelings now.
3. The loved one.
4. The environment, i.e., colleagues at work, neighbours.
5. The best that can be hoped for.
6. The thing that is most likely to go wrong.
7. Outcome.

Then try another few designations:
1. Yourself or the Questioner.
2. The home environment.
3. Chances for success at work.
4. Money.
5. Where your troubles are going to come from.
6. Where your luck is going to come from.
7. Outcome.

Engage brain before opening mouth

Give some thought to your Questioner and don't be too dogmatic about the cards. If the person sitting with you is young and single, their life-style and their view of life is going to be very different from that of a busy professional man or a retired schoolmistress. It is not cheating if you use a bit of common observation. I'm sure that you can tell, for example, if a person is nervous or worried. You could probably work out if they are like that because they are unfamiliar with having Tarot readings or because they have a lot of emotional and practical problems on their plate. Watch how the Questioner shuffles the cards, whilst sitting calmly yourself and creating a trusting and calm atmosphere. Don't try to be mysterious, just gentle and helpful.

Engage psychic powers before opening mouth

Try to 'tune in' on your Questioner, let your intuition guide you. If you get a strong feeling during the reading that this person is happily married but worried about his children, then say so. Let what wants to come come — if you open the door to your instincts, the magic will flow in. If you use the inner, instinctive area of your mind and don't allow self-consciousness to hold you back, you'll soon be on your way.

CHAPTER EIGHT

Calendar Spreads

The Annual Spread

The idea behind this spread is to give a reading for the next twelve months. The cards may be laid out in a straight line or in a circle. One, two or three cards can be used to represent each month of the year. In this case, I used two cards per month and laid them out in a circle as if I were placing them upon the hours of an imaginary clock.

In this particular reading I used all the cards in the upright position which meant that I had to bear in mind both the negative and positive influences contained within each card. As a rough guide, you can consider that the months which contain only Minor Arcana cards are ones in which the Questioner appears to rule his own fate, whereas the months with both Major and Minor Arcana cards show a mixture of control of events by the Questioner himself and control of him by circumstances. Months which contain only Major Arcana cards show the times when the fates seem to be ruling the Questioner. When using two cards together the Reader must look at their separate meanings and also a kind of compromise meaning. This could be a combination of the two cards involving a kind of reaction between the two cards as each affects and modifies the meaning of other.

Variations on a theme

After the reading is completed, another reading can be obtained from the same layout by using astrology. If this is to be done, the cards either need to be laid out in two rows or in a circle, with each card representing one of the astrological houses. (See Chapter 11.)

I would like to pass on a tip which was given to me by a Tarot reading

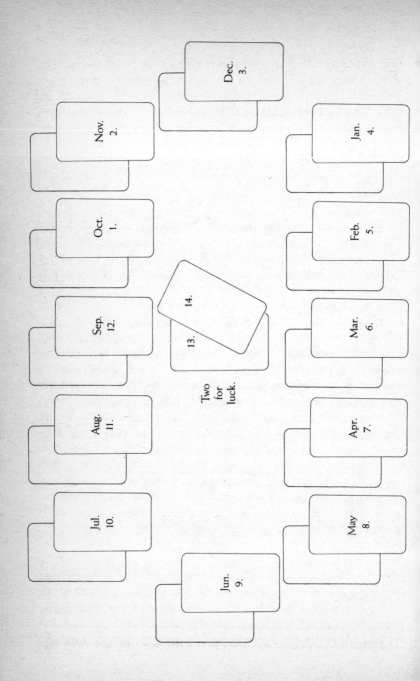

friend of mine called Lars Bratt on the subject of timing events. This shows how to use the suits of the Minor Arcana for the four seasons. He uses Cups for autumn, Coins for winter, Staves for spring and Swords for summer. I have not tested this theory out for myself yet, but it sounds as if it would work well; it has the right 'feel' about it.

The Annual Spread

Malcolm

Malcolm is a palmist who lives and works in a small provincial town. He has recently co-authored a book on hand reading which is called *The Living Hand*. He is tall, bearded, stately and slow-moving. A friend of ours once mentioned that he resembles Richard the Lionheart and, when I come to think of it, I can just see him in chain mail, a cloak and the white tunic of England. He is very kind, very gentle and very English: a lovely man.

We did this reading in the month of October, so that is where it begins.

1. *October* — The Emperor & Five of Coins
2. *November* — King of Staves & Page of Cups
3. *December* — The High Priestess & Knight of Swords
4. *January* — Two of Swords & King of Coins
5. *February* — Ten of Staves & Justice
6. *March* — The Chariot & Six of Cups
7. *April* — Ace of Cups & Five of Cups
8. *May* — Four of Swords & Wheel of Fortune
9. *June* — Death & Judgement
10. *July* — The Moon & Seven of Coins
11. *August* — The Fool & Ace of Staves
12. *September* — The Devil & The World
    Two for luck — Nine of Staves & Queen of Staves

The reading

October
The first two cards are the Emperor and the Five of Coins. The Five

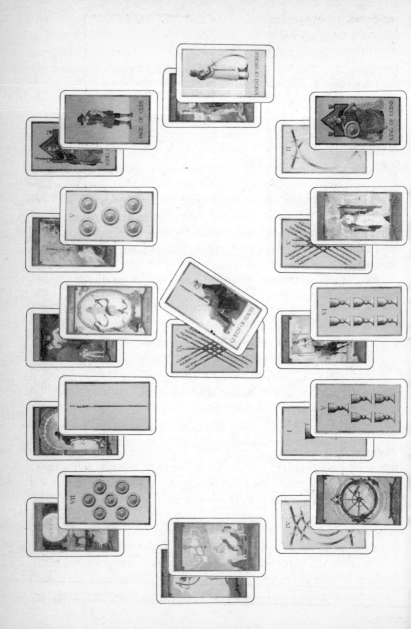

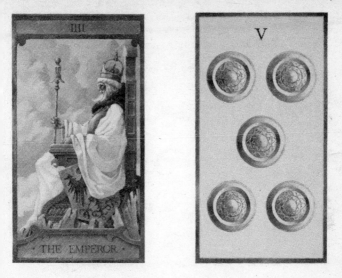

of Coins could indicate short-term financial problems but it could also throw some light on your state of mind right now, as it carries with it a feeling of being left out in the cold. You might see others around you having a good time and being happy while you feel left behind. The Emperor card often represents the boss, but in your case, being self-employed, you are the boss yourself. There is achievement and success here on the material level and a feeling that you are gaining more control of your financial circumstances, but the *emotional* side of life will be disappointing.'

November
'Here we have the King of Staves and the Page of Cups. This shows that you will be out and about among people in November and it will be other people who have the power to make you happy or sad. The King of Staves is a man who deals with and communicates with people for his living. He may be a salesman who drives around the country, a teacher, or someone who earns his living by talking directly to people. I see you as the King of Staves, partly because of your work and partly because of your appearance. (Malcolm is tall and slim with fair to grey hair.) The Page of Cups also has educational connections, therefore

KING OF STAVES   PAGE OF CUPS

I expect that you will be offered some kind of self-employed work in the field of education. Both the King of Staves and the Page of Cups indicate writing in some way, therefore written work may be important to you this month, possibly from this time onwards.'

December
'Here we have the High Priestess and the Knight of Swords. The Knight of Swords is a really powerful card. It seems to represent extremes; it holds within itself great energies, powerful forces for good and evil. The energy may be used constructively, in order to get things done quickly, or it may be used destructively in arguments and running around uselessly. There will be sudden and unexpected journeys. Something may break and need to be put right quickly — this isn't necessarily bad but it will require a sense of purpose. The court cards of the suit of Swords sometimes represent professional people, solicitors, doctors etc., therefore there may be a visit to one of these by you or someone close to you.

'The Priestess may represent one or more women who influence you at this time. On the one hand a woman may offer help in a manner which is coolly objective, or you could find that her senses desert her

and she becomes hysterical — especially with the energy which is shown by that Knight next to her. At any rate there seems to be pressure put upon you from a woman which could lead to decisive action in time to come. The Priestess also implies learning; sometimes learning the hard way, therefore you could learn some valuable lessons this month but you might not enjoy the experience. The Priestess is, of course, strongly associated with psychic work, therefore this card appearing on the eve of a new year shows that your road forward seems to be firmly rooted in this kind of work. You will, when in doubt, be able to rely on your intuition.'

January

'The next two cards are the Two of Swords and the King of Coins. The King of Coins might represent a man. This man would be of mature years and with either black or grey hair (formerly black). He would be well built and pleasant in his manner. Even if the description does not fit, the man would be a steady, sensible type of person in a settled kind of job or running his own business. The King of Coins is invariably money minded, materialistic but not necessarily mean. If this card represents a situation, then you will be reorganizing your finances, making arrangements which would offer you some kind of solid security for the future. However the Two of Swords means some kind of delay;

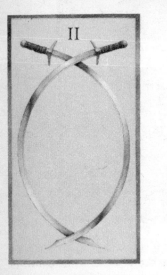

KING OF COINS

no movement in your affairs just yet. This set-up implies thought about your future, making some contingency plans but not doing anything drastic yet.'

February

'Now we have the Ten of Staves and the Justice card. The Ten of Staves shows that you will be carrying some kind of responsibility, taking on a difficult job and making an effort. I find that when this card appears, the job is always worth the effort. The Justice card shows that there will be benefits from this responsibility. You might be weighing up several possibilities but there will be at least a *mental* search for a more balanced and harmonious way of life. This is going to involve you in more work, more responsibilities and the Priestess which turned up in the December reading shows that this is likely to remain in the psychic field of work. You will be looking for a spiritual outlet via your work and balance in the whole of your life.'

March

The next cards are the Chariot and the Six of Cups. This might, on a very practical level, indicate a new car, or some work to be done

on your present car. On a deeper level, it implies *purpose* and the harnessing of opposing forces; the black and white horses on the card are supposed to represent opposing forces. These forces may be conflicting needs and desires within yourself, conflicting requirements among the people around you, and also your own energies being harassed in order to achieve something soon. On another level you could find yourself travelling this month as the Chariot does strongly suggest physical movement.

'The Six of Cups is a card representing the past and may mean that you are going to see old friends or go back to a place which has strong past connections for you. Your children, although no longer young, will be on your mind, and any arrangements you make now will probably include them in some way. (Malcolm has two grown daughters who are not yet financially independent.) You may use skills which you haven't used for a long time, and use them with a purpose (Chariot) or you may temporarily go back to a past way of life or a past manner of thinking. There is another side to the Six of Cups on an almost fortune-telling level; this can mean a family get-together or some kind of family conference. Obviously, therefore, you will not be making any important changes without family consultations.'

April
'Here we have the Ace of Cups and the Five of Cups. What a bitter-sweet mixture! This month will stir you up emotionally, that's for sure. Whether these cards imply new loves or old, I'm not sure. The Ace suggests that you might meet somebody new and important, but the Five of Cups is a card of loss and sorrow, therefore you may lose what you already have. The two cards are almost opposite in their meaning. The Ace is a card of love. It sometimes shows up before a Questioner receives an engagement or wedding ring, and it certainly shows great joy and happiness on the emotional level, but the Five is loss and sadness. The idea behind the Five is that three of the cups are lost and two remain. The remaining two give you something to build on for the future and indicate that not *everything* is lost. You could be pulled in two or more directions with some people around you offering warmth and affection and others causing you pain. A month of highs and lows, joy and anguish, possibly the beginning (Aces are beginnings) of a new way of looking at old emotions.'

May

The next two cards are the Wheel of Fortune and the Four of Swords. This, too, is conflicting and contradictory. The Wheel implies change,

a turning point, while the Four of Swords is associated with rest from strife, a holiday or some kind of time off. I suppose you could come to some decision while on holiday — it is hard for me to fathom this one out. The Wheel brings change — this may be because the Questioner causes things to change or because circumstances around him begin to change. It is possible that you could be propelled (Wheel of Fortune) into resting (Four of Swords). The Four does have another side to it, that being something to do with hospitals. I sometimes see this card in a spread before or during an illness but, oddly enough, it seems to be an optimistic card because it shows that if the Questioner becomes ill, he will be better soon. Sometimes people around the Questioner are taken into hospital. I've even known this card to mean that the Questioner is working in a hospital.'

June

'The next two cards are real humdingers! You have drawn the Death card and the Judgement card. I have never known the Death card to foreshadow the death of any Questioner himself, but I *have* seen it show up when someone around him dies, therefore it could mean that you will lose someone around you through death. On another level this card means the death of your present situation. In your case, this may be the point at which you and your friend split up: it seems to me from the previous cards that the relationship is on a road to nowhere, so this might be the end of it. There may, of course, be other, totally unforeseeable occurrences such as changes in relation to your work, or something completely out of the blue which I, with my minimal knowledge of you and your life, cannot begin to guess at. The Judgement card also implies an ending — I often describe it as a reward for past efforts, such as a "golden handshake" upon retirement. It *does* seem like a good ending, but in this case it might be a relief to have made the break — or even just to have made the decision to break. One way or another, this is going to be the month when some part of your present way of life dies off and something new begins. A "hospital" card followed a month later by a "death" card does suggest that someone around you will die after a short illness. I'm sorry to be the bearer of bad tidings, but it still could be metaphorical rather than physical. That's the problem with Tarot, you have to keep your options open.'

July

 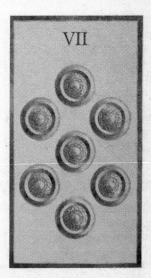

'The cards for July are the Moon and the Seven of Coins. The Moon is a difficult card to understand as it is associated with illusion. Its influence can make you view life through rose-coloured glasses and/or become upset and emotional about nothing. Moonlight is confusing, romantic and mysterious. Under its influence, some things may suddenly come to light — you may find yourself able to understand the motives of others or the circumstances around you far more clearly through intuition than you would by logical thought. The Seven of Coins is a strange card as it can indicate slow growth on the one hand and forlorn hopes on the other. Once again, there is a warning here to try to get things straight and not to make any binding arrangements which may not suit you in the long run. You may unravel some mystery or suddenly find yourself able to put your finances into some sort of new order. There is a strange feeling that this is the time when you could, through some chance meeting or strange accident of fate (Moon), get the chance to begin some project which will build up slowly for the future (Seven of Coins). Women could both help and hinder at the same time. There is another oddity here and that is the Moon's connection with water. This could pull you towards water, towards the sea in some way.'

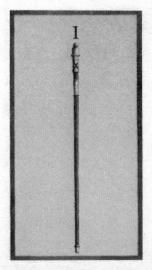

August

'This month brings you the Fool and the Ace of Staves. This is definitely your new beginning, firstly because all the Aces indicate new beginnings and, secondly, because the Fool is definitely a fresh start with new doors opening. Staves are associated with negotiations, business matters, teaching, writing and learning, travel and communications of all kinds; therefore the Ace indicates new beginnings in this area. This card is associated with *birth*, either in the real sense that there may be a new baby coming into your circle, or in the sense of the birth of a business, a change for the better with new opportunities which create a rebirth of your personality.'

September

'Here we can see the Devil and the World cards. Well, Malcolm, you may think that you will have given up sex for good, but this combination tells me that any self-denial will only be temporary! The Devil card has quite a few meanings but it is often associated with sex. It is mainly a card about commitment and, as it is laying alongside the World card, there seems to be a commitment to something new following the completion of the old. The Devil is quite a creative card but also practical in nature — let's say that he is associated with basic necessities rather than spiritual growth. The World is an optimistic card and, like the Moon, is also associated with water, in this case with travel over or sometimes towards water. It seems that there will be a new world for you which will require commitment. This could come in the form of a new job or business or possibly a commitment to a new personal relationship. There is *no* evidence to show you buying a new house, none of the property investment cards have yet come up, but you may rent property for a while. It is quite interesting to note that most of your cards have been leading us towards changes in your life which are personal and practical in nature, possibly involving a move to a new area working in a new way and meeting new people; this spiritual side will also be important this year.'

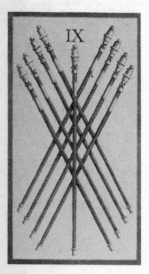

Two for luck
'I am putting two cards in the middle to give a summing up and to add some final flavour to the reading.

'The first is the Nine of Staves which shows that, despite the changes which seem to be coming, you will end up on fairly firm ground. The idea behind this card is that you will be holding your own but will have to take care that unforeseen circumstances don't topple you into trouble. It might be a good idea to take out some kind of health insurance or to make sure that your investments are secure. Nothing is going to drop into your lap — you will have to work at life in order to achieve anything — but you should be able to make something worthwhile for yourself. There will be enemies and jealousies to watch out for, but nothing you cannot cope with. You will also find yourself surrounded by problems on occasions, unable to move out of their way.

'The last card is the Queen of Staves. Well, it would have to be a woman, wouldn't it? You have quite a few women around your life one way and another and your year ahead will be bound up with them. The Queen of Staves could indicate business negotiations with a woman or even a business partnership. If the card signifies a real-life person then she will be slim with brown hair and a bright and breezy manner. If this card represents a situation, then business matters will be successful, especially those which involve travel and communications.'

After the reading

Very often, after I have finished a reading, I turn to look at my Questioner only to find him or her miles away, lost in thought; this was the case with Malcolm. I asked him what he thought of the reading and he answered that most of it made sense, the bits which he didn't know about would probably fall into place in a few months' time. There was no doubt that I was seeing the end of a relationship followed by a move — very likely to a town by the sea. Malcolm told me that in October he would be taking a stand at an exhibition where others (mainly women) would be joining him, so he would be acting in the capacity of 'boss', just as the cards said.

Some of the predictions were not so immediately obvious, however he said that even these made sense to him. He saw that he might have to renovate or even replace his car and he would have to look at his finances before making any major moves. He could see himself travelling in connection with work, but at the moment was not sure whether the Death card meant that somebody would die or that his circumstances would 'die' in some way: he suspected that there could be a bit of both. All in all, he remarked that it showed that he had a lot to face up to during the coming year and would let me know the outcome.

This spread can be laid out in a circle, a line or series of lines, whichever is the most convenient.

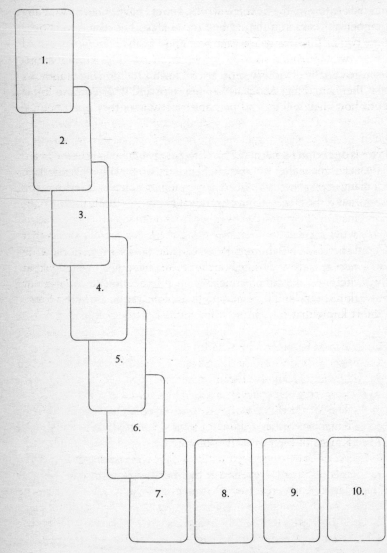

The Ten Weeks Ahead Spread

This is virtually the same as the Annual spread but is applied to the immediate future, the next few weeks. I could have gone forward any number of weeks, but ten seemed reasonable. The idea is to choose one, two or three cards for each week and analyze them. As usual I chose two — that seems to feel right somehow. This kind of short-term reading is obviously most useful for a Questioner who knows that there are things about to happen soon and who wants to know both how they will go and perhaps exactly *when* they will occur.

Peter

Peter is on the point of leaving his wife, ostensibly for another woman. The fact of the matter is that he has been unhappy within his marriage for many years. The children are now reaching independence, his wife is well aware that the end is nigh, and fate was just waiting for the right combination of circumstances to nudge him into action. The 'nudge' came when he met another lady just a few weeks ago. It seems that Cupid shot his bolt and our Peter became fatally smitten. Now he has a *reason* to leave and some hope for future happiness. We hope that the switch-over will all go amicably. As it happens, Peter is also out of work just now and is beginning to explore various business ideas. I didn't know that side of his story until after the reading.

1. Ace of Coins & The Chariot
2. Page of Coins & The Empress
3. Queen of Coins & Death, reversed
4. King of Cups & Seven of Staves, reversed
5. The World & Nine of Staves, reversed
6. Knight of Staves & Nine of Coins, reversed
7. Knight of Swords & Two of Staves
8. Six of Staves, reversed & Eight of Staves, reversed
9. Ace of Swords, reversed & Eight of Cups, reversed
10. Ten of Cups, reversed & Strength

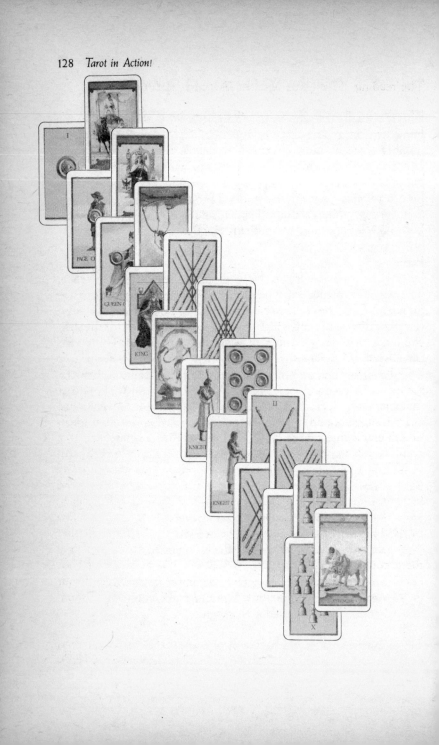

The reading

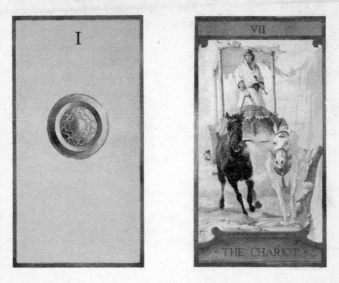

Week 1

'The first card is the Ace of Coins; all aces mean the start of something, but this suggests a business or work-related matter and often foretells of self-employment. You have also picked the Chariot, and the combination of those two cards would mean that you are on the point of starting a new career. The Chariot is sometimes a card of travel but it always signifies doing something with a purpose and it can send you travelling abroad or driving round this country, but its main indication is that it's marshalling opposing forces; this being signified by the different colour of the two horses which are pulling the Chariot. There are many ideas passing through your mind at the moment and there could be a split between your conscious actions and your unconscious requirements. You must take immediate charge of your own life and your own circumstances and make a start quite soon.'

Week 2

'Here we have the Page of Coins, which means that a child or children could be an issue now, particularly one child — dark-haired, fairly

PAGE OF COINS

III

THE EMPRESS

stocky, cautious, practical. Bad behaviour is not really in the character of the child but it could either become ill or badly behaved, due to nerves at this time. The child is close to a woman represented by the Empress, and it appears to me that the Empress is your wife, because this card shows an interest in family matters, the home, garden, money and the apparent stability of the past, therefore she could be concerned about her status, survival and also what will happen to the child or children. The Empress also tells me that you've got to concentrate on practicalities yourself, particularly practicalities associated with the home, land, the base and what you're going to live on.'

Week 3
'The Queen of Coins — this is a business woman or a businesslike woman and is probably Anne (girlfriend) who is a business-minded, practical-minded person. The Death card is next and this represents the death of a situation, an ending which clears the way for something new. It really means transformation as one phase ends and another begins. However this card is reversed and that creates a delay. You may want to make this move but might be held up by circumstances;

you could even have second thoughts. You will also lose some of your old friends as you change partners.'

QUEEN OF COINS

DEATH

XIII

Week 4

KING OF CUPS

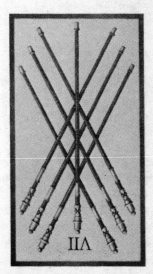

VII

'There are people everywhere: you have picked Court cards right, left and centre and now here is another one. This is the King of Cups who is a man who is middle-aged or older, helpful, kindly and on your side. He could give you good advice; he may be a relative or friend. The Seven of Staves which is reversed now shows that an embarrassing situation could arise and this again rather shows a hold up. If it were upright, you would be able to sort out all the challenges and problems around you quickly, but being reversed it tells me that you can't do much about it. In the event, the person represented by the King will stand by you, even if he is in the end somewhat ineffective because the Cup people are not really strong when it comes to a fight (especially when on someone else's behalf).'

 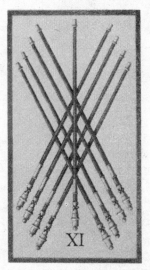

Week 5

'This card is the World and does not show a sudden change but more of a developing situation. It could be the end of your world as you know it and the beginning of a new one. It is an outward-facing card: it pushes you out from the boundaries to see what's beyond those four walls. I feel that getting a job, the right job, is something that's going to be on your mind over the next few weeks because you've picked the Nine of Staves which is reversed. This shows that you are not settled yet but you may be looking around, going for interviews and talking to people. Because the reversal of this card shows that you are not on firm ground, you are becoming increasingly free to choose a new life for yourself, but it is unstable and insecure at the moment.'

Week 6
'Here we have the Knight of Staves which is more likely to mean a move of house than a person, also the Nine of Coins which is reversed. The Nine is often associated with buying furniture when it is upright, selling goods and furniture when reversed; therefore one could assume that this is the beginning of arrangements to sell up, move out, etc. The selling side is emphasized by the reversed Nine and the action of movement by the Knight. There is as yet no indication that you will immediately buy another property.'

Week 7
'We have here the Knight of Swords and the Two of Staves. The Knight coming right after the other Knight means movement in your affairs,

KNIGHT OF SWORDS

doing things with a purpose. Sword cards also indicate professional people — doctors, solicitors, etc. — therefore, this looks like a particularly active time for you. The Two of Staves indicates a partnership, either in business or friendship. Staves indicate conversation, negotiation and communication, also in this case property, therefore you could rent or buy something new soon as the negotiations seem to be beginning now. There may be the start of a new job or business here, too.'

Week 8
'This definitely shows arrangements being made because we have the Six of Staves which is reversed and the Eight of Staves which is also reversed. Obviously the reversals here show that there could be setbacks, delays and problems of a practical nature. The Eight could indicate jealousy and spite coming towards you, so you must expect some kind of nasty letter or other kind of unpleasantness from a source of jealousy. There is a slight warning not to go ahead with any business matters too quickly and also not to travel too far just now.'

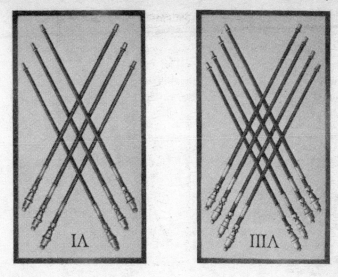

Week 9

'Here we have some advice as to how to tackle the problems as we have here the Ace of Swords and the Eight of Cups and they are both

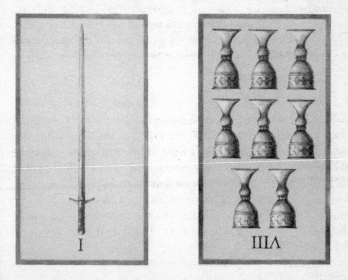

reversed. This shows that, although you must take charge of your life, you mustn't go at it like a bull in a china shop. Keep your temper, watch what you are doing. You will have more power than you realize, even if it is only the power of veto. The Eight is a really good card as it shows that you are celebrating at this time. Although this is only a few weeks away, there seems to be something to celebrate and be happy about.'

Week 10

'You've got the Ten of Cups which is reversed and the Strength card up here. The Ten of Cups is the wish card, especially where emotional matters are concerned and, even if it's reversed, you are due to get some of the happiness that you are looking for. There is a little sadness wrapped up with the happiness because the Ten of Cups is a family card and with any split up, however well deserved and needed, there is always a little sadness and regret. The Strength card is symbolic as it means *gentle* strength. It does augur well for your own health and strength, and there is very little here to suggest that you would be ill in the coming weeks.

'It does put you in a strong position — a stronger position than you think. This shows that you must make an effort to be fair over the divorce and to be, in a sense, magnanimous in victory. This also tells me that your own energy will no longer be sapped by this situation and you will be able to store up energy for yourself now, sleep better, etc. This card when reversed so often means a sort of emotional anaemia where the emotional strength is draining away from the person, but upright, as the card is in this spread, it is a kind of emotional tonic medicine. It's the beginning of the build-up mentally and spiritually for your future.'

After the reading
There is no real postscript to this reading as all of it related to circumstances which Peter knew were due to occur and, as to the actual train of events, the next ten weeks will give us all the answers.

Some months later
Peter is now living with Anne in her house. He is working for an insurance company.

How to Look at the Week or Fortnight Ahead

It can sometimes be useful to look just a week or two ahead by using a variation of the ten weeks ahead spread with one or more cards for each day. A pal of mine called Jean Goodey uses a simple idea just to see whether any earth-shattering events are likely to occur to her clients in the immediate future. To be fair, Jean only uses this when she realizes that changes are fairly imminent in her client's life.

Jean takes the Major Arcana cards only, gives them to the Questioner to shuffle and then puts them down in a series of twos, usually with one card crossing over the other. If the Wheel of Fortune turns up in this layout it shows that there *will* be major changes and on what day they will occur. I tested this out on myself a moment ago, knowing that nothing major was going to happen over the following couple of weeks (as far as I know!). The spread involves laying out twenty of the twenty-two Major cards, therefore the Wheel ought, by the law of averages, to turn up somewhere — it didn't, it was one of the two cards which didn't appear. A quiet couple of weeks ahead then!

CHAPTER NINE

Comprehensive Spreads

The Pyramid Spread

This spread is called the 'Pyramid' because of its shape. The base line can be any convenient number of cards — usually seven. The spread can be used to give a generalized reading or can be focused upon a particular problem. There is no specific area of life allotted to each of the positions, but it is usual to use the base as the background to the situation and then move up the Pyramid in order to move forward in time.

In the case of this reading, I did not concentrate on any one point but allowed the cards to lead me in the direction which *they* chose. I used four cards for the base line, then three for the next row, then two, and finally one at the top. As the reading did not seem to end on a particularly conclusive note, I took one more card in order to create a satisfactory conclusion. This is perhaps a good way of showing that one doesn't have to adhere strictly to *any* spread, and that it is always appropriate to follow one's instincts when reading Tarot. In this case I also laid the cards face downwards and turned each one over as I progressed with the reading.

Laura

Laura is a neat and attractive woman, small and slim and now in her middle forties. She is at a crossroads with both her personal and working life, and her children are reaching independence. She is going to make a number of far-reaching decisions over the next year or so, therefore the reading could be expected to show changes and to direct those changes towards the most pressing factor.

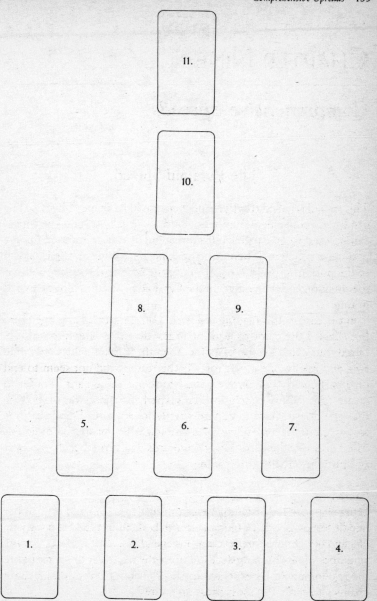

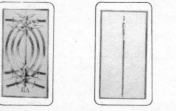

1. The Sun
2. Six of Staves, reversed
3. The Hermit
4. Three of Cups
5. Seven of Swords, reversed
6. Ace of Staves
7. King of Swords
8. The Lovers
9. The World
10. Page of Cups, reversed

Extra card — Death

The reading

I laid out the cards in the Pyramid shape face downwards on the table.

'I shall read the cards from the base upward starting at the left-hand corner and working towards the right. It seems logical to do it this way.

'The first card is the Sun card which, in addition to its usual meaning of happiness and of harvesting the good things of life, also indicates to me dealings with children and young people. It seems that the greatest joy in your life has been your relationship with your children.

'The second card along is the Six of Staves and it's reversed. This shows me that many battles have been lost in the past: you have probably worked hard and tried a number of things but none of them have come to a worthwhile conclusion.

'The third card is the Hermit which shows tremendous inner loneliness in the past. You seem to have felt completely alone even though you were living in the middle of a family.

Laura
'Yes, that is so.'

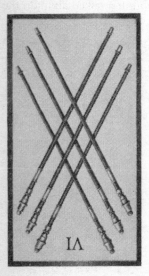 

Sasha
'The Hermit is facing towards the Sun card and the small light thrown by that little lantern is travelling across the Six of Staves towards the Sun card. This shows that, despite past battles, you have found some kind of inner light plus great feelings of understanding between you and your children.'

Laura
'I would agree with that.'

Sasha
'The Hermit suggests that you have been centering yourself, travelling

on an inward path. You have been developing spiritually and working out who you are and where you want to be going. It shows a search for your own identity and your own philosophy. You may have drawn strength from yourself and from people who think along similar lines to yourself.'

Laura

'Yes, that is so, I have made good friends at work.'

Sasha

'The card on the end of the base line is the Three of Cups. Has there been some kind of wedding or celebration talked about in the family?'

Laura

Shakes her head and looks puzzled.

Sasha

'Nothing like that at all?'

Laura

Shakes her head again.

Sasha

'OK, it means that we have to read this card on a different level, a less practical and a more symbolic level. One way of looking at this is to say that when the children actually settle down and get married, your duty to them will be over. You've got sons, haven't you?'

Laura

'And a daughter'.

Sasha

'But no weddings yet. Right, well it seems as if the cards are saying that although your life has been bleak in parts,' pointing to the two centre cards, 'the Hermit and the Six of Staves reversed make a bleak centre to this line, but the outer cards show that there have been outside pleasures and happiness from people outside of the home.'

Laura

Nods.

Sasha

'Let's move forward a bit and see where you are heading in the near future.' Turning over the left hand card on the second row: 'This is the Seven of Swords and it is reversed which shows that in practical terms you are going to have to cut your losses in some way. You will have to leave something or some part of your life behind and make a fresh start with what you have left. It is worth mentioning that this card often indicates talking to a solicitor.

'The second card is the Ace of Staves which is a very strong card indicating a birth. This is, in appropriate cases, the birth of a child, but often means a metaphorical birth or rebirth in the life of the Questioner. It shows that it is time to branch out and look for new avenues and new ways of living.

'The next card is the King of Swords. In a literal sense this would indicate a man over the age of forty. This is often a professional person, especially a doctor or a lawyer. As we don't seem to be dealing with health in this reading, I suggest that this will be a solicitor. This is a particularly purposeful card which, taken together with the Ace of Staves, shows a great move forward on your part soon.'

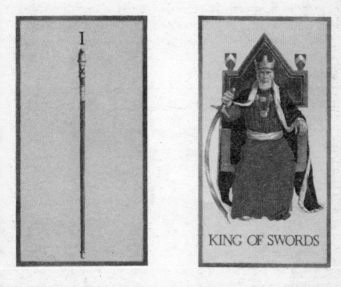

KING OF SWORDS

Laura
'Yes, that makes a lot of sense.'
Sasha
'OK, let's go on now: the next two will take us further into the future.' As I turned over the next card we both giggled a bit because it was the card of the Lovers. 'The Lovers card can imply love and sex but

it is mainly about choices and decisions and, as the card is the right way up, it looks as if you are going to make the right decision. It is also worth mentioning here that this card shows decisions which affect people who are close to the Questioner and often suggests joint decisions and family choices. The "book" meaning of this card is the choice between sacred and profane love. I can tell from this card that you *do* have a lover in the real sense of the word. The Ace of Staves has phallic connotations in any case, therefore love and sex will be a part of your future life. The Lovers card shows beauty in its many forms and, apart from the beauty (in your eyes) of your loved one, there is an indication here that you will shortly be improving your own appearance and buying some new clothes. The picture shows, in addition to the lovers and Cupid, the tree of knowledge and some mountains in the background. The tree implies all kinds of knowledge, not just sexual knowledge, and the mountains show that you have some journeys yet to make, journeys in fact and journeys of the spirit too.'

Laura

'That sounds right.'

Sasha

'Yes it does, doesn't it. The card next to the Lovers is the World.

That has a picture of a girl dancing inside a wreath of leaves. Now in the Jewish tradition bagels are served to mourners at funerals. These rather sweet bread rolls are ring shaped, rather like doughnuts, and they signify the endless chain of life, showing us that even as one person dies, others must live to create the future. This card always reminds me of that particular piece of symbolism. It also means that you will soon achieve an ending to some part of your life and a feeling of completion, even of satisfaction, before beginning on the next phase. It is now time to look outwards from your home and marriage towards all the other options, to all the corners of the earth which are symbolized by the astrological images on the card of the lion, eagle, bull and water carrier. This is often considered a travel card and may indeed be so in your case. You will see more of the world and meet a greater variety of people than you have before, and the optimistic nature of this card leads me to believe that this will be of a great change for the better.

'The last card will show us the outcome. Here we have the Page of Cups and it is reversed. Cups are associated with love and affection, also Pages are often one's children, therefore you could miss the children and have a slightly lonely time ahead of you. The whole-hearted love you are seeking with the Lovers and the World may not be immediately available. This card is also a card of education but, as it is reversed, it is perhaps not a time for learning but a time for action. You may also have some doubts about the man, your "lover", as to his reliability where your future is concerned. Another feature of the Pages is that they can suggest a move from the married to the single state, and in your case the reversed placement of this card shows either a delay or a reluctance in proceeding with the parting or in actually divorcing.'

Laura

'This all makes sense to me.'

Sasha

'As the last card wasn't all that conclusive, I think I will take one more for luck.' I took a card from the top of the deck. 'Look! Here is the Death card. This does not mean that you are about to die, of course, just that your present way of life is about to die. Sooner or later there will be a complete change of circumstances based on the matters which we have been talking about. There's no denying that life is going to become unfamiliar and very different in the future.'

After the reading

I found myself staring thoughtfully at the cards for a while.

'You know,' said Laura, equally thoughtfully, 'that Sun card is right. About the only worthwhile thing that came from my marriage has been the children — there are four of them by the way. I am still under the influence of the Hermit, still thinking about the future, still not sure which is the right thing to do.'

Laura pushed the cards together into a heap. 'There is a man friend, of course; the cards were quite right; oddly enough *he is a solicitor.* He is not married and is willing to live with me, but I'm not sure. I'm not sure that I want to live with anyone for a while. I need some time to be alone.'

'The Lovers card shows that he cares, Laura,' I said. 'He will have to be told of any decisions you make. The children will have to be consulted too.'

'Oh, of course,' said Laura. 'They are practically adults now, but even so, I would discuss any changes with them beforehand. I can see the relevance of the new beginnings, the death of the old and the birth of the new. It all seems quite cut and dried doesn't it?'

'What is wrong with your marriage, Laura?' I asked softly.

'Dick has always been violent; he used to have a mania about religion when we were younger too. He has never had a sense of proportion, schizophrenic I suppose; but with four children, there wasn't much chance of escape.'

'It looks like there soon will be.'

'It certainly looks like it,' Laura smiled.

Postscript

It appears that, around the time that I gave Laura that reading, she had a couple of other readings done by other Readers and in each case she had been told that she must get away from her husband before he hurt her really badly. My feelings were that she wouldn't actually make her move until it was too late. It was that reversed Page of Cups that I didn't like. It showed me that she was refusing to learn from past experience and wasn't facing reality. The Death card which followed on after the Page made it clear to me that she would have to be catapulted out of the home by some kind of irresistible force.

As it happens, there has been a rather incredible turn of events since I last saw Laura, which goes to show just how strongly two people can be linked when they have a psychic connection. Soon after the new year, I found myself thinking of Laura. Each time I saw her face in my mind I felt a tremendous hot pain high up in my right thigh. This made my right leg so weak when it occurred, that I actually found myself staggering around the room. After a few days of this, I had a dream in which I was told to get in touch with Laura. I rang her home and spoke to her son who told me that she was in hospital; he gave me the address so that I could write to her.

As soon as I put the phone down I had a vision in which I could see Laura being pushed down the stairs and, as I saw this, I felt a strong push on my own left shoulder, a bump on my head and a crashing pain in my right hip and thigh. I wrote to Laura and told her what I had experienced and that I was sending her love and healing thoughts. She replied that the 'accident' had occurred exactly as I had visualized it and that the right femur was so badly broken that she was having it pinned. Meanwhile, she had lost her job and had no means of supporting herself while she learnt to walk again. Her husband was regularly visiting her in hospital and trying to get her to come home again as he couldn't understand why she was leaving him! She may have to go back; she has no other place to go.

The Romany Spread

This is probably one of the oldest spreads in existence; however it is more often used with playing cards than with Tarot cards. It doesn't give much help to the Reader because it neither points the cards to specific areas of life as, for instance, does the Celtic Cross, nor does it include any other form of divination or symbolism which might give added clues to the Reader.

To prepare for the reading, ask your Questioner to shuffle or stir the cards and then choose three lots of seven. These are placed in three rows which represent the present, the past and the future. I came across a similar spread in a very old book which was lent to me by my friend, Barbara, but that spread used thirty-six cards and each one was given a designation, such as 'affection', 'faith', etc. Frankly, I thought the ordinary version was hard enough without trying to fit half a deck of cards to such a large collection of rather old-fashioned ideas. However, I am grateful to Barbara for the loan of her book as it showed me that there is, as far as I can tell, no better version of this spread than the one I have used here.

For this reading I used the cards in both the upright and reversed positions, and did not choose a specific significator.

Bethany

Bethany is a tall, slim, attractive, blonde lady in her mid-thirties. Her character is interesting and unusual and her life story so far would be enough to keep the average TV soap opera going for years. Bethany has had a very good education which has enabled her to obtain high-level jobs in the scientific side of the business world. She has been married and divorced twice with one child, Emma, from her first marriage and two children, Mark and Elizabeth, from her second marriage. She has a full-time nanny, Colette, who helps her to run the home. She divorced her second husband, Tarquin, last year because

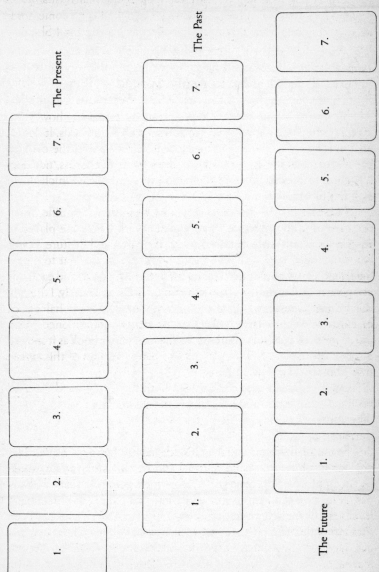

The Present

7.

6.

5.

4.

3.

2.

1.

The Past

7.

6.

5.

4.

3.

2.

1.

7.

6.

5.

4.

3.

2.

1.

The Future

he was living more or less permanently with another woman. She left her previous job a few weeks ago and has just found another one. She owns her own small home and therefore, although her salary is high, her financial needs are as great as any man with a young family and a stay-at-home wife. She still makes herself responsible for her (recent) ex-husband's family and their problems and, as if all that were not enough, she has just been told that she has cancer of the gall bladder.

The present
1. Justice
2. Two of Staves
3. King of Staves, reversed
4. Ten of Staves
5. The Star
6. Five of Cups, reversed
7. Six of Coins

The past
1. Seven of Cups
2. Five of Coins
3. Queen of Cups, reversed
4. Wheel of Fortune, reversed
5. Six of Cups
6. The World
7. Eight of Staves, reversed

The future
1. King of Coins
2. Seven of Swords
3. Seven of Staves
4. Knight of Cups, reversed
5. Nine of Coins, reversed
6. Eight of Coins, reversed
7. Strength

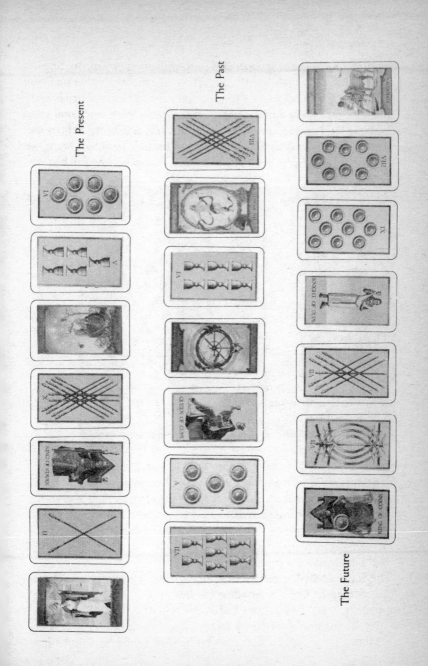

The Present

The Past

The Future

The reading beginning with the present

Position 1
'The first card is the Justice card which, on one level, can imply that there are legal documents to be signed, and on another level it shows that you are striving to find some sort of balance in your life and to harmonize matters.

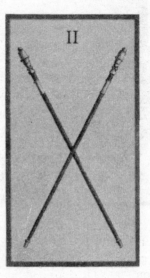

Position 2
'There seems to be a partnership, a mental partnership, a combining of ideas with somebody else. This is the Two of Staves. It also shows that you have the chance to make decisions which will affect yourself and others. Sometimes this signifies a proud man in your life.

Position 3
'The King of Staves, reversed: this looks to me like your potential new boss. He looks like a man who tells lies.'
    Bethany said, 'I know he's a liar.'
    'Yes, he certainly looks shifty, rather incapable; shifty and fat-headed.'
    'I know he is,' agreed Bethany. 'Fat-headed would be about right.'

After a moment's thought, I said, 'He appears to have no sense of honour, there is this sense of trickery about him. He's not a very capable man.'

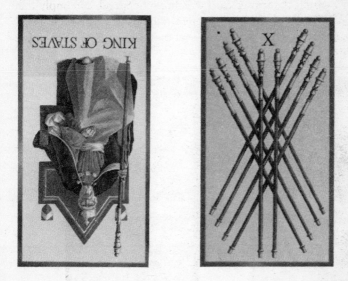

Position 4

'You're going to be asked to take on a lot of responsibility; you are taking on a lot of responsibility in your life anyway, this is shown by the Ten of Staves here. You are carrying all those burdens, particularly those living in your home. However, because the card is upright, you will get there in the end. You are carrying these burdens willingly, and there is a feeling of reaching the end of a road eventually.'

Position 5

'The next card is the Star, the Star of Hope, as I call it. This is an optimistic card, so despite the fact that you are supposed to be dying of a terrible disease, I can't see it. Also, although the guy in this new job is going to cause you trouble, you've got to go through this because something else seems to come out of it. This is also an occult card, so there is a growing of psychic awareness now for you.'

Position 6
'The next card is the Five of Cups, reversed — you are getting over
a broken heart, the bad feelings are slipping into the past gradually.

There doesn't seem to be a complete loss. You will still see something of your friend and still have friendship but not a complete relationship.'

Bethany nodded her head.

Position 7

'Here we have the Six of Coins which is the pay-out card. I think you will be earning good money, you have a lot of paying out to do, but you *will* have the money to do it with. You can earn it but there are so many mendicants around you that you finish up giving most of it away.

'This is interesting; if we take another look at this first part of the spread, you have only got two Major Arcana cards here which means that you can direct your own life at the moment. Also there are three Stave cards together which means negotiations, business work, travel.'

The past

Position 1

'It seems that you have done a lot of things in your life. Even discounting any previous lives which you might have had, you've done plenty of living this time round. You have looked at a lot of options and tried a lot of pathways. This is shown by the Seven of Cups here. You haven't got the answer yet.'

Position 2

'You've now got the Five of Coins which, to my mind, always carries with it a feeling of being out in the cold. You have done a lot, you've earned money, but you have finished up out in the cold. You've kept the home fires burning, but not been allowed to sit at them. This situation has been caused by others. You've been looking for emotional fulfilment, but looking in the wrong place.'

Bethany answered, 'They say that about women executives; they say that they can go out and earn the money but will never be fulfilled emotionally.'

'I think that's true to some extent of men as well, but they seem to be able to concentrate wholly on their career without feeling the lack of closeness. They can get away with leaving wifey at home with the children, apparently completely content — and if she's got a lover who keeps her sweet, then it works even better,' I replied.

Position 3

'Now the Queen of Cups, reversed here, in the past: I think this is yourself here. This is not a sad card but an unfulfilled card; sadness in the past.'

Bethany broke in, 'I think this is my sister, she has had a very hard time of it.'

'Has she?' I replied, 'There's been sadness and unhappiness there too, hasn't there.'

'Yes.'

Position 4

'The Wheel of Fortune, reversed here, so things have been very much against you. Things have happened to you and around you which have all been pretty disastrous.'

Position 5

'There is one good thing here — you have had good relationships with your children, I can see that from the Six of Cups here. Also you have probably had quite a good childhood yourself. If you were to think back a long way, you probably didn't expect the reality of marriage to be as bad as it was. You probably got a bit of a shock when faced with the reality of it.'

Bethany almost shouted, 'Yes, absolutely true! No way when I was younger could I have foreseen this. I always imagined that I would have this wonderful marriage with six children. Never dreamed that I would go out into the world to be a business woman.'

'I can see that you must have been shattered by it all,' I sympathized. 'However, there are skills from the past which will come in handy in the future. You've a good education behind you.'

Position 6

'The World card shows that you have made a world for yourself, you have climbed up from your sea of problems. You've travelled a bit, met a lot of different people and learned a lot and you have created a worthwhile world for yourself. A world of your own, associated with your children.'

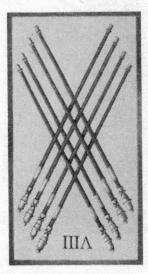

Position 7

'The Eight of Staves, reversed: you have probably had the potential of travel rather than the reality. In some way, this seems to contradict the World card a little. You could have earned more and done more if you had been able to emigrate somewhere. Also you have had a lot of jealousy and spite directed towards you in the past, even from both of your husbands.'

The future

Position 1
'Now we have here the King of Coins. This is a man, could be anything, let's leave it at that for now.'

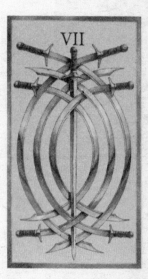

Position 2
'The Seven of Swords: to some extent you're cutting your losses and moving along, you're leaving behind the marriage that didn't work, the jobs that didn't work and the past that didn't work; gathering up your remaining resources and moving on. Also this should be the end of the legal ties and problems.'

Position 3
'We've got another Seven here. I think that the Sevens are quite

purposeful — there is a slight feeling that you are going out and taking on the world. The Seven of Staves indicates the separation of one's problems into bite-size chunks and tackling them one by one.'

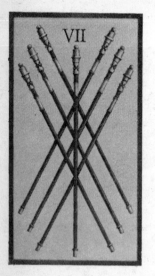

Position 4

'This is the man you wanted, the Knight of Cups, reversed. He's gone but is still around you.'

'Yes,' said Bethany. 'I still see him around me but he does not want a relationship.'

'That's right, he is afraid or unwilling to make a commitment, but that man we drew out first, the King of Coins, would make a commitment and he is perhaps yet to come.'

Position 5

'The Nine of Coins, reversed: this is your difficulty in financing the home, I think. Sometimes I find this card appearing when people are getting rid of furniture, so you may be parting with some stuff which needs to be thrown out. This is not the time to build up financial commitments, to have debts hanging round your neck.'

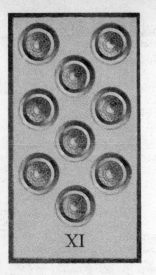

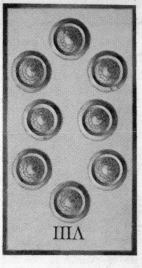

Position 6

'Now the Eight of Coins, reversed. This is the new job, and it will only be for a short term. If you take this as being a monthly reading this would give you about six months, yes? It's not really going to work out.'

Position 7

'Here is the Strength card. Your health and strength will hold out. I don't think you've got cancer — I think you've got something all right; but not cancer. If it really is cancer, then it doesn't seem to be the galloping variety. I don't see you dying or even having a lot of dealings with hospitals at the moment. There are very few health cards here.'

Bethany pointed to the King of Coins, 'Can I make a suggestion here? This King could, I think, be Emma's father, my first husband. He has just come across with her school fees and seems to want to help me to help her with finances anyway. He is a businessman, he has his own company.'

'Yes,' I replied, 'that would fit, practical help from a businessman.'

After the reading
We chatted generally for a while and agreed that the reading had accurately reflected Bethany's life. I truly couldn't see any real indication of major health problems, but as to that plus the other future events, we shall have to wait and see.

Six months later
Bethany has had a major sortout in her job, adjustments have been made and the situation is now clearer and better. She had her gall bladder removed — it was abnormal but seems to be presenting no more problems. Her 'Cancerian' friend did slide out of her life and her first husband has helped her a bit. Bethany moved house again and is now living in the depths of Surrey.

CHAPTER TEN

Comprehensive Spreads Allied to Other Forms of Divination or Symbolism

The Astrological Spread

This spread is based on the idea of the astrological houses, and it is popular with those professional Readers who are also astrologers. Most professionals are familiar with other forms of divination in addition to the Tarot, and they may incorporate some of these ideas into their Tarot readings. I was an astrologer and palmist before becoming a Tarot Reader, therefore it was easy for me to incorporate the house positions into my readings.

I would like to offer a word of warning here, and that is that Tarot has a knack of subtly changing everything that it touches, and that is also true of this concept. Astrological techniques do not work in exactly the same way in Tarot as they do in astrology, but the *ideas* which are contained in each of the astrological houses are basically the same.

This is not the best spread for a complete beginner to use as there is too much to remember, but if you are already familiar with Tarot, use of this spread will enormously increase the depth and scope of your readings. I have included a 'quick clues' section which provides the Reader with the main points of this spread in an easily digestible form.

The value of this reading is its ability to cover almost every aspect of a Questioner's life in one viewing. It draws the Reader's attention immediately to the most interesting and problematical sections of the Questioner's current situation.

Position 1

This represents the Questioner, the physical body and what happens to it; therefore it shows the current or recent past state of health and circumstances. The Questioner's mental and emotional state may show up here. People who are of special interest to the Questioner at the time of the reading often show up here in the form of Court cards. The manner in which the Questioner is acting and expressing himself at the time of the reading could also be seen here.

Position 2

This represents money and possessions: one's personal fortune (or lack of it) are shown up here — anything that the Questioner values, both things of value and matters of priority or moral value; matters related to farming, gardening and the land, plus building; also artistic matters such as music, dancing, singing, drawing and painting. Some important relationships show up here and, in the case of these, money dealings will be an important factor.

Position 3

This represents the local environment, matters under negotiation and, in some cases, papers to be signed. Local journeys, travel to and from work and vehicles generally are to be found here. People represented by this position are likely to be of the same generation as the Questioner or younger: these may be brothers and sisters, brothers or sisters-in-law, neighbours, friends and colleagues, also — although this conflicts with pure astrology — children and young people. All forms of communication including telephoning, writing, public speaking, etc., are here plus most kinds of education, including self-education. Again, unlike astrology, I have found exam results, even the driving test, showing up here. Foreign languages, sports and games, buying and selling are here — this position is really concerned with day-to-day communications and all kinds of written and verbal interaction between people.

Position 4

This represents the private side of life: the home, property and premises of all kinds; domestic life, roots and background; parents, especially the mother or other older females who stand in the place of the mother; the instincts and any remnants of childhood behaviour or phobias.

Position 5

Here we find children; fun, holidays, entertainments and gambling; above all *lovers;* creativity, personal projects, self-employment, the Questioner's own business and other speculative matters; the stage, drama and dancing.

Position 6

Duties and day-to-day service to others are represented here. This usually relates to work, but may include chores around the home. Superiors and subordinates, everything related to health, doctors, hospitals, hygiene, etc., are also found here.

Position 7

Partnerships, relationships, husband, wife, etc., occupy this position, as well as lovers, if the relationship is settled enough. Open enemies, close business colleagues and business partners also feature.

Position 8

This position contains two ideas. The first is of jointly administered funds or money gained and lost through others, (ie, legacies, mortgages, taxes, alimony, corporate (business) matters, banking, investment, etc. The other side involves intensity and transformation, ie, intense feelings, both one's own and those of others, and sexual matters; birth and death, beginnings and endings; a sense of commitment; renewal and regeneration, transformation; the mediumistic side of the occult. Anything that is deeply hidden — even mines and mining — is covered by this, and any situation which transforms two people into three or two into one.

Position 9

Expansion of the Questioner's horizons, eg, travel, higher education, new environments; foreigners, foreign goods and business matters relating to long-distance travel; publishing; the law, important legal documents and court cases; religious, philosophic and mystical matters;

the occult (possibly more important in this position than in the 8th); sporting matters, fresh air pursuits; gambling on horses; the need for personal freedom.

Position 10

This represents the aims and aspirations of the Questioner: usually the career but this may relate to political, domestic or creative aspirations. Parents, especially the father and father figures, are found here, as well as status, ambitions, responsibilities and professional standing, public attainment and success.

Position 11

This position represents political and humanitarian ideas, group philosophies; social life, clubs and societies, friends and acquaintances; detached relationships and intellectual pursuits; hopes and wishes and the chances of achieving them; conversation; learning for pleasure.

Position 12

Here we find inner thoughts and feelings, fears, self-imposed limitations or hidden resources and abilities. Association with hospitals, prisons and asylums may be seen here, as well as the Questioner's real inner desires, the subconscious mind; self-sacrifice, escapism, negative and positive emotions which either give great support to or tear apart the Questioner from within; secret projects, secrets in general; hidden friends and enemies; psychic matters, the mystical, the occult.

Quick clues to the Astrological Spread

NB: The Astrological Houses are also the equivalent of the Signs of the Zodiac.

1. Aries	7. Libra
2. Taurus	8. Scorpio
3. Gemini	9. Sagittarius
4. Cancer	10. Capricorn
5. Leo	11. Aquarius
6. Virgo	12. Pisces

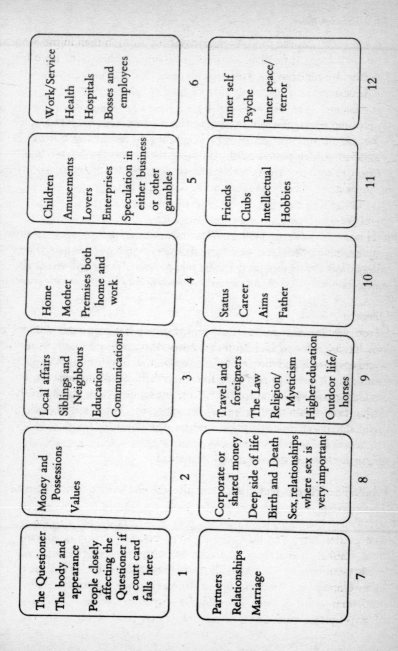

| The Questioner
The body and appearance
People closely affecting the Questioner if a court card falls here

1 | Money and Possessions
Values

2 | Local affairs
Siblings and Neighbours
Education
Communications
3 | Home
Mother
Premises both home and work

4 | Children
Amusement
Lovers
Enterprises
Speculation in either business or other gambles
5 | Work/Service
Health
Hospitals
Bosses and employees

6 |
| Partners
Relationships
Marriage

7 | Corporate or shared money
Deep side of life
Birth and Death
Sex, relationships where sex is very important
8 | Travel and foreigners
The Law
Religion/Mysticism
Higher education
Outdoor life/horses
9 | Status
Career
Aims
Father

10 | Friends
Clubs
Intellecual
Hobbies

11 | Inner self
Psyche
Inner peace/terror

12 |

Astro-Tarot

This is a spin-off from the Astrological spread. It shows how the spread can be extended in order to extract further information. The first thirteen-card spread (the Astrological spread) should show the Questioner's present position or that which is just coming into being. When you have finished giving this reading go round the spread a second time with twelve cards (omitting the one-for-luck card) and see how things develop. After that, you can concentrate on any areas of the spread which appear to be particularly important to the Questioner. For instance, if the Questioner wants more information on the future of his job, place extra cards on the 6th and 10th positions. If he wants to delve further into relationships, then place cards on the 5th for lovers, 7th and 8th for all aspects of any love/marriage relationship. Travel prospects can be placed upon the 3rd and 9th, and so on.

Derek

Derek is an unusual person by any standards. He is tall, thin and would look elegant even in sackcloth and ashes. He has brown curly hair, an engaging smile and the piercing blue eyes characteristic of his Scorpio Sun sign. He peers at one over the top of little gold-rimmed, semi-circular specs. He came to this country some years ago from New Zealand and hasn't yet become acclimatized to our ice-age weather. He qualified as a doctor and then became interested in hypnosis. He now works as a hypnotherapist and psychotherapist and he has recently written a very good book called *Hypnosis*.

Problems with the reading

This reading seemed to go completely wrong. Derek couldn't relate to any of it, but after a few moments' reflection he could see it applying to events which he could envisage taking place in a couple of years' time. This was one of those readings which show the Tarot cards acting as a kind of 'event-seeking missile'. If there is nothing drastic going on in the Questioner's life at the time of the reading, they *seek out* the nearest interesting point in time. They look for areas of conflict and times of major effort; this is why it can sometimes be difficult to see the

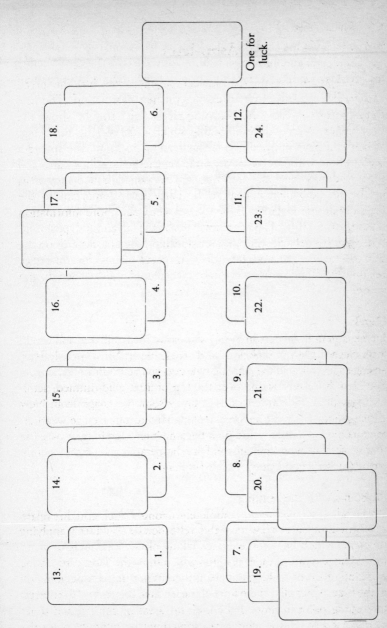

One for luck.

future because the cards keep looking back to some event in the past.

In this case, I couldn't get a reading for the *present*: the cards seemed to consider Derek's current situation rather boring, and were much more interested in the financial locational and emotional changes which are in Derek's future.

I offered to do the reading again, this time asking the cards to tune in to the present, but Derek suggested that we leave things as they were and see what happens in a couple of years' time. In any case, the primary purpose of the reading was achieved, and that is to interpret the cards as they fall. This reading also goes to prove that, although Derek and I are acquainted, we are not close friends and I don't know anything about his private life, therefore the reading stands or falls on the merits of the cards which he drew.

The first spread
1.   Wheel of Fortune
2.   Judgement
3.   Six of Staves, reversed
4.   King of Coins
5.   Knight of Cups
6.   Three of Staves, reversed
7.   Two of Staves, reversed
8.   The Empress
9.   Eight of Cups
10.   Page of Staves, reversed
11.   The Hierophant
12.   Eight of Staves, reversed
One for luck — Four of Cups, reversed

The first spread.

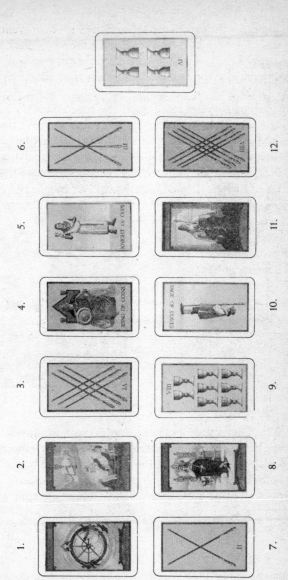

The reading

One for luck

'This is the Four of Cups, reversed, which is showing new friends, new doors opening, pastures new, new experiences and probably quite a lot of satisfaction in life just now.'

Position 1

'The Wheel of Fortune, especially in this position, shows that you are making changes or facing changes in your life. It is important to look at the ratios at this point because there should be two of the Minor Arcana for each of the Major Arcana. Therefore, in a spread like this with thirteen cards there should be five Major and eight Minor. Let's see what we've got: one, two, three, four Major cards, so things are rather more in your own hands than in the hands of fate.'

Position 2

'Judgement. Something is coming to an end here to do with money.'

Derek laughed. 'That's true, I haven't got any.'

'That's right,' I answered, laughing, 'your money's coming to an end.

'This has more to do with how you organize your money. Possibly there is some sort of payment or something to come. You're changing direction, changing the way you organize yourself and changing the way you think about money. Your priorities are going to change as are the priorities of people around you.'

 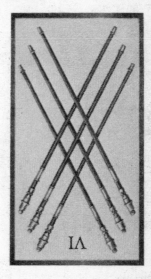

Position 3
'Now the Six of Staves, reversed, and this tells me that you are trying to communicate with people around you — relatives, friends — and getting nowhere: there is a lack of understanding. This could be due to distance, or just that you and others are on a different wavelength.'

Position 4
'The King of Coins: this could be an element of yourself, but I can't see you as this particular King. It does mean that your home and even your office, which is an extension of your home, is very firmly rooted. There may be money invested in property and that's probably the only security you've got at the moment. You should not under any circumstances enter into any dubious business schemes where you lose your security. However, you may be entering into a partnership

with someone who is shorter and heavier in appearance than yourself
— grey-haired and rather money-minded, wealthy, quite helpful, but
conservative in outlook and different from you.'

KING OF COINS

KNIGHT OF CUPS

Position 5
'The Knight of Cups, reversed, could mean that if you have children
from your previous marriage you may find it difficult to keep in touch
with them or difficult to communicate with them in some way. Children
could be an obstacle in your life and you may find yourself having
difficulty in reaching an understanding with them. If that doesn't apply,
then I think your love life is in difficulties at the moment because it's
hard to get any sense out of anybody or to put your point across. Your
best bet really is to concentrate on work and business and to push
forward in that direction.'

Position 6
'The Three of Staves, reversed, shows new projects, new ways of
working, but these are hard to get off the ground; things will go very
slowly for you at first.'

Position 7
'Here we have the Two of Staves, reversed. This just repeats the whole property and partnership situation.'

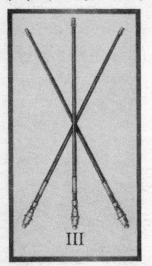

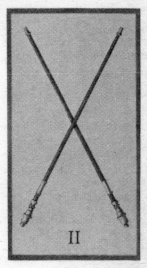

Position 8

'Here we have the Empress. This shows that there will be eventual fulfilment and your plans will come to fruition in the end. This also points to satisfactory relationships with women in the future.'

Position 9

'This is the Eight of Cups which makes me think that you've turned your back on New Zealand for the time being, but I've got the feeling of a journey with a certain amount of sorrow involved.'

Position 10

'This is the Page of Staves, reversed. You seem to be making arrangements, telephoning, writing letters, but the reversal of this card again shows delays, indecision, frustration. This could relate to work situations or to worries concerning the health of one of your parents.'

Position 11

'The Hierophant here shows that your friendships will be among more conservative people — people with a traditional outlook. It is interesting to note that this position shows friends and groups but also shows one's dearest wishes and hopes. The Hierophant is sometimes a card of marriage, therefore you could hope to be married again soon.'

Position 12

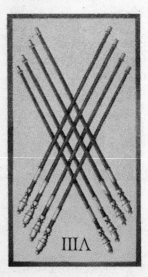

'Now the Eight of Staves, reversed, which often indicates travel but, as it is reversed, it suggests delays: you want to travel perhaps but can't yet. There can be a feeling of loneliness here too, as if everyone else has friends and someone to love, but you are being temporarily left out. You could be envious of others.'

The second spread

I then put out another twelve cards on top of the previous twelve (omitting the one for luck).

1. Nine of Coins, reversed
2. Seven of Cups
3. Two of Swords, reversed
4. The High Priestess
5. Queen of Coins, reversed
6. Page of Cups
7. Seven of Staves, reversed
8. King of Staves, reversed
9. Four of Swords
10. Ten of Swords, reversed
11. Ace of Cups
12. Queen of Staves, reversed

The second spread.

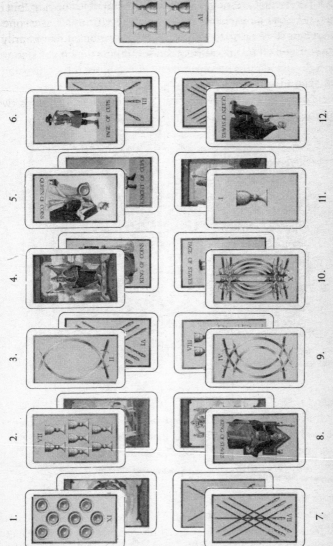

Position 1

'This card is the Nine of Coins, reversed. Strangely enough, I find that this card shows up when people are selling furniture, getting rid of things, possibly prior to a move. This may point towards property being foisted off on you rather than something which you choose for yourself — you must be very careful not to move into something you don't like just for the sake of expediency.'

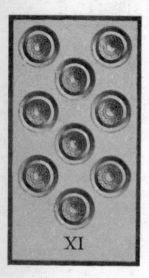 

Position 2

'You have the Seven of Cups here which shows financial confusion. You will be looking at a whole load of options, savings, spending, investments. You seem to be really turning over in your mind various values and priorities.'

Position 3

'The Two of Swords, reversed here is just repeating the fact that there will be problems and misunderstandings in the area of negotiations. There could even be a problem related to vehicles, local travel.'

Position 4

'The Priestess in this position shows that you will be studying again, whether this is in your own field or something else, I don't know. You will be studying at home, reading, learning, understanding. There are times when you are perhaps too intellectual, too liable to theorize, but perhaps this is just a temporary phase.'

Position 5

'The Queen of Coins, reversed in this position, suggests that there are, or will be, dealings with a woman. She is very dark haired, very attractive and could be somewhat money-minded, either because she needs a high standard of living or because she is rather hard up. She could be either too down-to-earth or totally impractical, either way she will think in a different way about these things than you do. This is going to be romantic, even wildly romantic for you. There will be problems with this relationship, practical problems. I think it's possible that she has a child, and there could be problems surrounding this. She will in some way be allied to your work, very keen on what you do. She has some experience of the same kind of work and would perhaps wish to work with you. She is not a theorizer, not a mental type of person;

she is warm-hearted and down-to-earth. She needs stability, the practicalities of day-to-day life to be smooth and satisfactory; she is a family person in many ways, loving but possibly a little calculating.'

Position 6

'The Page of Cups here suggests that you will have to learn how to work in a new way or to cope with a new kind of work. This card alone could be the most important of the whole reading. There is possibly a very slight suggestion of a child being ill here.'

Positions 7 & 8

'Now, with the Seven of Staves reversed and the King of Staves which is also reversed, I again foresee a partnership which could be awkward or embarrassing in some way.'

Position 9

'This is the Four of Swords which is also reversed and this means that I have to ask you a question now. Are your parents well or is one of them ill, because I've got hospital for a parent?'

Derek answered, 'My mother was in hospital which is why I went to New Zealand over Christmas.'

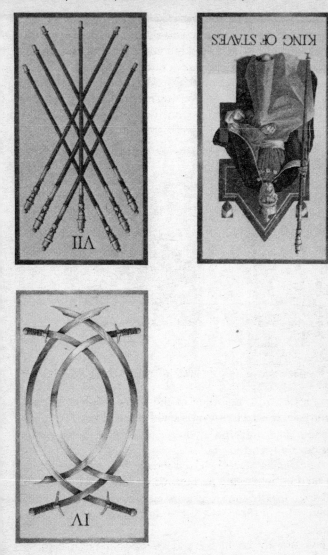

'Oh, well, the card doesn't imply death thank goodness, just something which needs to be put right.'

Position 10
'Now the Ten of Swords, reversed, and this too suggests a set-back
with reference to your work. I think you are trying to set something
up in some way and it just doesn't work out straight away. This won't
be complete abandonment but just as if your plans . . . I've got this
again and again, it seems that whenever you have to work with someone
else, there's something standing in your way.'

Positions 11 & 12
'There is another woman here represented by the Queen of Staves,
reversed. She is someone whom you see as a friend, but she wants
to be more than a friend to you.'

The third section, extending parts of the spread
I continued down the deck and took a few more cards in order to clarify
certain points. Out of these six cards, four turned out to be Major
Arcana cards.

The third section.

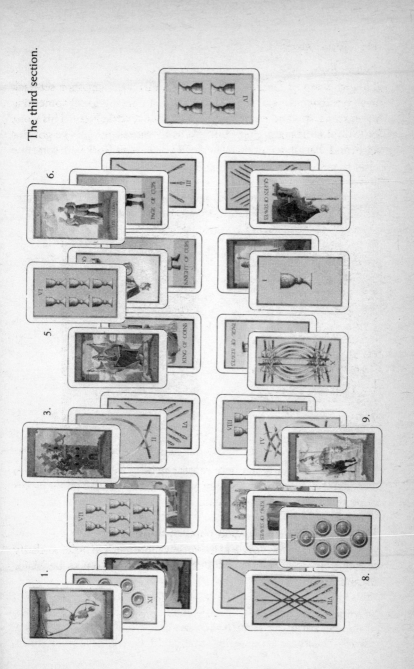

1. Death, reversed
3. The Tower
6. The Lovers
5. Six of Cups
8. Six of Coins
9. The Chariot

Position 1
'Now we have the Death card, reversed, which shows that you are hanging on, waiting for some situation to be changed.'

Position 3
'This is the Tower which always implies some kind of shock coming at you out of the blue, a house tumbling round one's ears. It's as if a letter will come which will jolt you out of your present existence and into a new environment.'

Position 6
'Here is the Lovers card which shows a choice or decision in the realm of work, also there is the feeling that decisions will have to be made

by a group rather than by you alone in the future. You could also work with someone you love.'

Position 5

'Here we have the Six of Cups. You could be going back to a previous relationship or meeting someone similar to a previous girlfriend. The past is going to be important. I'm pretty certain that whoever it is has got a child or children.'

Position 8

'Now the Six of Coins. Once more we see a re-think of your financial priorities — money to be obtained and then spent for a purpose.'

Position 9

'Now the Chariot. I am going to change my mind about travel. I said that you wouldn't travel soon but that is wrong. I think that you have no *plans* to travel at the moment but that you will do so; you will have to take off very quickly. This is the card of opposing forces, and this position of the spread is related, among other things, to philosophy; therefore, you are going to have to sort out your own philosophy of life plus the requirements of others.'

After the reading

Derek gave a kind of list of his comments and reflections.

'A few facts. I'm not really in a partnership, medically. I have a colleague and we send each other patients, but no partnership. There will be a change in his premises arrangements soon but I don't see that he can do me in the eye. As far as property or finances are concerned, I have no property — I'm buying a house, but that's all I have in the world. I can't see that I am going to get into financial deals because I'm not interested in that sort of thing. My attitude to money is always minimal — I really don't think much about it. I may have to think about it as I'm running out of money, but I don't see myself being involved in any financial concerns or being asked to leave my house.

'My love life? Well, I'm still very attached to a girl in New Zealand and this may be the one you're talking about because she does have children. My hope is that, in the future, I will go over there and marry her. You talk about something happening suddenly: the only thing that could happen is if her situation changes and she asks me to come over to her.'

While Derek paused for thought, I said, 'I still think that something to do with premises or property will change suddenly. You see, the cards can be very fickle, sometimes they go back in time, sometimes forward — they look for the nearest important point. The lady in New Zealand is in the background and cannot be with you, can she?'

'She's now studying hypnosis,' answered Derek. 'At the moment I'm taking out a doctor over here, but I don't feel terribly romantically involved. Perhaps you are talking about that one?'

'No,' I replied, 'it's New Zealand. The lady doctor is someone you can talk to and share the same wavelength with — she's just a friend. I have to warn you that she cares for *you* more than you care for *her*. You see her only as a friend. I feel that your young lady in New Zealand is going to ring you and tell you that her circumstances have changed. You will then have to unwind the whole deal that you have got here and that will be the beginning of the events which are the reading.'

'Well, Sasha, there is a man who wants to start a clinic, a kind of centre, in New Zealand.'

'That looks like it, doesn't it? We'll have to wait and see.'

The Crowley Spread

This method of reading Tarot is so complicated that it is probably nigh on impossible to do properly. The actual reading which I have demonstrated is only for the *first section of the whole thing* which, in itself, is an incredibly full reading. This was given to me by my friend, Peter, who in addition to being the subject of the reading, is also a lover of the Tarot.

Section one — the Tetragramaton
This section is based on the Kabbala and uses the four letters of the Hebrew name of God as its basis. The first step is to nominate a significator, then ask the Questioner to shuffle the cards and cut them into two piles using the left hand and moving towards the left. Now ask him to cut each of the two piles once more; again using the left hand and moving towards the left (see page 192). Now you must find the pack which contains the significator. If it is in the second pile for instance, ask the Questioner if his most pressing problems are truly represented by the pile that the significator is found in. If the answer

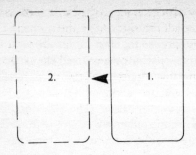

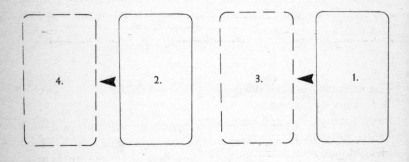

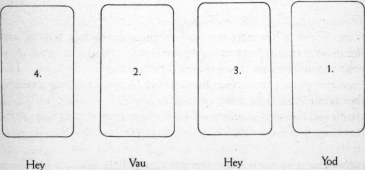

Hey   Vau   Hey   Yod

is yes, then you can proceed to read the cards, if the answer is no then you must gather up all the cards, give them to the Questioner and tell him to start the procedure all over again from the beginning. If the Questioner agrees that the sphere of life belonging to the pile which contains the significator *is* correct then you can proceed with the reading.

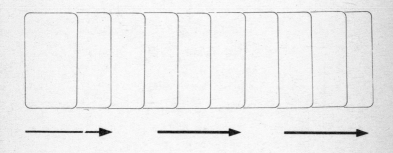

The relevance of each pile
Yod: Work or business.
Hey: Marriage, love, pleasure, sex.
Vau: Loss, disputes, troubles.
Hey: Money or materials problems.
Assuming that you have now found the right pile, take the cards one by one and read them off in one long line.

Section two
This time, deal out the whole pack in a 'clock' formation of twelve piles. These piles represent the astrological houses. Locate the significator by clairvoyance or by dowsing!* If it doesn't turn up at your second attempt, then abandon the spread and go back to the beginning of the whole thing and start again! If you do manage to locate the significator, then read the pile in which it is found as per its astrological house significance. I have given a full description of the meaning of the astrological houses on pages 166 to 169.

* Dowsing using a pendulum, rather like water divining.

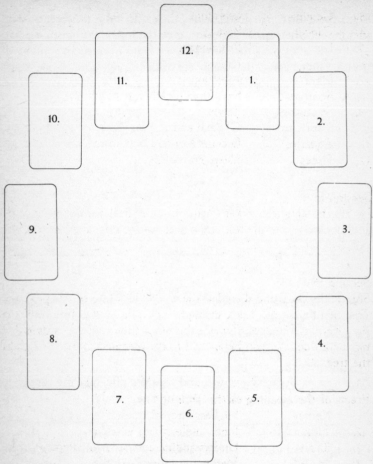

Section three
This section is almost the same as the previous one, and you have to set about it in exactly the same way. However, instead of the astrological houses, we have the signs of the zodiac with a rather old-fashioned version of their meanings.

1.   Aries   Anger.
2.   Taurus   Beauty.

3.	Gemini	Learning.
4.	Cancer	Rest.
5.	Leo	Prominence.
6.	Virgo	Labour.
7.	Libra	Affection.
8.	Scorpio	Sex, birth, death and psychism.
9.	Sagittarius	Travel.
10.	Capricorn	Old age and responsibility.
11.	Aquarius	Eccentricity and occultism.
12.	Pisces	Sleep, mysticism.

Section four
Locate the significator, keep it to one side, deal out thirty-six cards anti-clockwise, put the rest of the pack to one side, and just read the thirty-six cards.

Section five
Shuffle the cards and then deal the whole deck into the shape of the Tree of Life spread. Look through each pile of the Tree until the significator is found (don't dowse this time), then read the cards in that pile with due attention being paid to the meaning of that branch of the tree.

Precis of the meaning of the Tree of Life

1.	Kether	Highest internal quest.
2.	'Hokma	Inner intellect and wisdom.
3.	Binah	Understanding and outer intellect.
4.	'Hesed	Mercy and inner emotion.
5.	Geburah	Judgement.
6.	Tiphareth	Beauty and essential self.
7.	Netzach	Love, passion and sex.
8.	Hod	Business, politics and communications.
9.	Yesod	Foundation and ego.
10.	Malkuth	The home and body.

A full reading for the Tree of Life spread follows in the section of the book which has been specifically set aside for it.

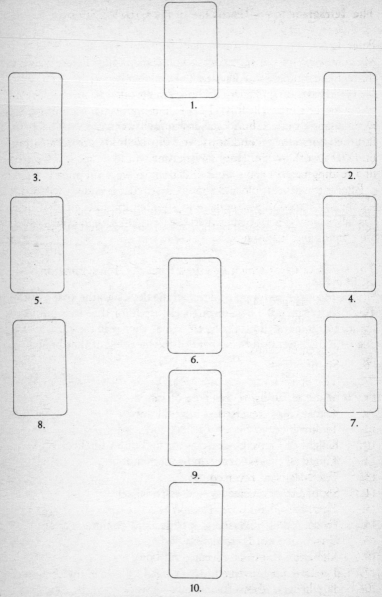

1.

3.

2.

5.

4.

6.

8.

7.

9.

10.

The Tetragramaton — Part One of the Crowley Spread

Peter

My guinea-pig for this spread was a young man called Peter. We went through the shuffling and piling routine and then found the significator. We could have just looked for this, but Peter is a dowser and he decided to dowse for it himself. If he did not find it after the second go, we were supposed to start shuffling and cutting all over again. As it happens, it turned up on the second dowse and the pile told us to concentrate on Peter's working life. Peter said that he would be most interested in a reading based on his work situation, so we went ahead.

Peter is thirty years old and happily married. He and his wife work for the same recording company in London. He told me that he is basically happy in his job but would like some insight into events which are coming into being now.

The string of cards which emerged from the Tetragramaton

1. Three of Cups
2. The Hanged Man
3. The Empress
4. King of Staves, reversed
5. Queen of Coins
6. Six of Staves
7. The Star
8. Seven of Coins, reversed
9. Ten of Cups, reversed
10. Temperance
11. Knight of Cups
12. Knight of Staves
13. The Magician, reversed
14. Six of Cups, reversed
15. The Hierophant
16. Ten of Coins, reversed
17. Queen of Swords, reversed
18. The High Priestess, reversed
19. Two of Cups, reversed
20. The Lovers, reversed

21.   The Fool, reversed
22.   The Devil

The reading

'I see a great deal of joy here: this is the Three of Cups which usually means a celebration, great joy, sometimes a marriage. You mentioned that you and your wife work for the same company, and that shows a sense of commitment both towards each other and towards your work. You seem to have a sense of real joy in what you are doing. You might have the occasional off day, but on the whole you must enjoy your job immensely.

'The Hanged Man is the second card, which could indicate that you're waiting for something; you could be suspended between two spheres of your work — there is a possibility that your role's going to change. There is a feeling of great spiritual satisfaction in your work rather than just the material aspect, and I know that this is an awfully stupid thing to say, Peter, but I'd bet you'd almost do it for half the money.'

'Yes,' replied Peter, 'absolutely.'

'You enjoy it so much because it gives you satisfaction and also because it gives you a chance to help other people.

'We've now got the Empress, and this too shows a feeling of achievement, fruitfulness and great satisfaction in the production of the records. I don't think it's business for business' sake, I think that the actual product gives you a great deal of pleasure.'

Peter nodded.

'Now we have the King of Staves, reversed, and this is somebody that you may be working with; someone who is a potential or an actual boss; he is definitely among the men around you. If it is a person, I have to describe him as being slim, over forty, possibly not a terribly good communicator in a verbal sense, and he could tell lies for the sake of trying to please people. He is the type who would make a promise in order to keep somebody happy while they're standing in the room with him, then later on go back on it.'

Peter laughed and actually broke out clapping! He went on to say, 'This is my immediate boss, who is a Director of the company and is very unwilling ever to tell the Managing Director the truth, even though the Managing Director desperately likes to know the truth of the situation. And this is also partly why I get on so much better with the M.D. rather than with him. I can tell my M.D. the truth and he will appreciate it even if it is not what he wants to hear.'

I continued with a bit more information about Peter's difficult boss. This then is a man who tells people what they want to hear because he is a probably a bit of a coward when having to deal with people face to face. He is also a clever person and I feel that he has missed his vocation in some way. He feels that he could have, and probably should have, got a whole lot further up the ladder of success. He has hang-ups left over from his childhood; he would like to be the boss of the whole business but he hasn't got the business acumen to do it. Frankly, Peter, he's a slippery customer. On a social level he could well be quite pleasant, but this slipperiness and cowardice causes you some sort of danger.'

'Not really danger, more a constant irritation which stops me getting on with the job sometimes.'

'Well,' I said, 'I would treat him as a mushroom, if I were you.'

'A mushroom?'

'Yes, keep him in the dark and feed him plenty of horse manure.' Peter curled up laughing, 'Love it!' he exclaimed, 'Love it!'

QUEEN OF COINS

'Next to him and probably connected to him we have the Queen of Coins. If this is a person, she could be of any age, but most probably is middle-aged and dark-haired, fairly well built. This woman is very materialistic, money-minded — she has to know what's coming in and going out. If she is not an actual person, then this might be something to do with the finance department and the budgeting which is also not at the moment working in your favour. There could be collusion or misinformation between these two here.'

'Sasha,' interrupted Peter, 'this is very odd, because the wife of the man whom you have described is the personal assistant to the Financial Director of the studio.'

'Crikey! I'm doing well today, Peter!'

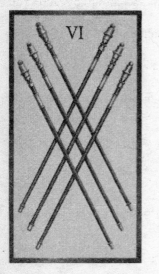

'Now I have the Six of Staves which is a very good card: it represents a victory and achievement so I should think that you could find a way to manoeuvre around this problem. If we go back to the Empress here which is an achievement as well, this shows that you could find a creative way of crawling around this situation.'

Peter nodded in agreement.

'Well, there's your significator, the Star. The Star is a card which is associated with achievement and learning, with pushing the boundaries of experience and understanding outwards. They say, don't they *"per ardua ad astra"* — through hardship to the stars?'

'Do they? I don't know that one.'

'I'm surprised Peter, it's quite a well-known saying. It means that hard work will get you there — I'm not sure that that's true, a bit of old-fashioned guile needs to be added to the hard work in my opinion.'

'Very true.'

'Anyway, the Star represents hope, optimism and faith in the future. You're reaching out as far as you can go and you're not quite sure where it's going to take you.'

'Life's an adventure.'

'Yes, that's right, Peter. This is such an optimistic card.

'The next card throws a certain amount of cold water over you as it is the Seven of Coins, reversed. This represents unfulfilled hopes of some sort. To some extent, you may overreach yourself Peter, and that "certain something" which you are particularly hoping for is not going to work out. On the other hand, it can mean slowly forward, slowly forward. Then we've got the Ten of Cups, reversed. When upright, this is the nicest card of all as it means emotional fulfilment but, as it *is* reversed, it is putting a shadow on this fulfilment. You will be moving upwards in the company hierarchy and will no longer be involved in the part of the job that you like.'

'It's an interesting situation,' said Peter. 'There is no doubt that since my job has become more administrative, my goals have become different as well. Whereas before, the pleasure came from working in the studio, now it is from actually succeeding in getting the music through its production schedule on time.'

'You're going from tactics to strategy.'

'I'm having to re-align my goals so that I can actually enjoy achieving them.'

'The Temperance card next; this shows that you will find a way of coping with everything. I call this the recipe card because you get a large bowl, toss everything in, mix it up and it comes out as a cake.'

Laughter from Peter.

'Well, it's the mixing of fine elements, it's the alchemy card. What you have to do is to turn yourself from a person who produces records into an executive — it means weaving a little magic around yourself in order to do this.

'Now, this could help you: here we have the Knight of Cups and the Knight of Staves. These are probably some young people, some young blood coming into the company which will give you the opportunity to build a little power base of your own. The only thing that worries me about the Cups is that there is often a little bit of idleness attached to them, that you might tend to leave for tomorrow what you should be doing today.'

Peter let out a small sigh, 'Yes, that's quite true.'

KNIGHT OF CUPS

KNIGHT OF STAVES

'Therefore, if you are moving on to a higher level of work, there will probably be one or two idealistic, enthusiastic youngsters who will fulfil the role which you formerly filled yourself — the dreamer's role.

'These two youngsters have rather different personalities: one of them would be softer, slower, inclined to enjoy food and drink; the other sharper, a bit sarcastic perhaps, brighter and with more of an eye on the main chance. Although the brighter one will look like a better bet than the other one, remember Cups represent water and that will settle into all sorts of odd places and will often do very nicely for itself in the long run without having to expend much apparent effort.

'The Magician, reversed, well you are going to find this change of roles a little difficult to start with. Despite the fact that a book reviewer recently criticized me for seeing the Magician in a business context, I really do find this card is allied to work matters. You may have to bury the mystical side of yourself slightly and discuss work with people who have far less understanding and less awareness than you yourself have. The Magician is also to do with skills and it shows that you might have one or two skills missing which you will have to do something about. You are certainly very good with people, a skilled negotiator and good at getting most of what you want, but there's something practical missing here: maybe you need to learn how to use the office computer.'

'That's quite interesting,' said Peter, 'because, if it relates to the recent past, I can accept that. Two weeks ago I went on a training course to use a new sound synthesizer. We've had it in the studio for weeks, but I didn't know how to use it.'

'OK, so you're tackling that, sorting out a missing skill. The Magician also implies some kind of trickery which may be used against you so you must bear that in mind as another possible interpretation.

'This one is the Six of Cups, reversed, and it always says to me "don't go back to the past". Once your young staff have been trained, let them get on with the job, don't do it for them. Delegate, don't interfere. The skills you once had are not going to be useful to you in the future, so you must let other people do things their own way — you can advise them but you can't do their job for them.

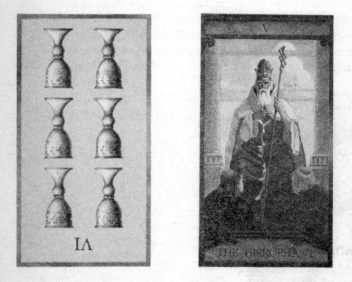

'Ah, now the Hierophant. You are moving upwards, you are going to be in a traditional business role from now on. Also with this card you must be seen to be like Caesar's wife. You have to be *seen* to be doing the right thing. You must be *seen* to be honest, totally fair.

'Now we have the Ten of Coins, reversed. This is a bit difficult because, if it were upright, it would be the start of something big. You may, on a very practical level, be getting a raise, because this might be a small amount of extra money. Secondly, you will definitely be a little unsettled in your new role. Another possibility is that it may not be so easy for you to get on with the financial departments as it is to get on with the artistic and creative side. The budget side may be difficult.'

Peter said, 'That seems too to be a situation which is already on the boil because, personally, I believe that the members of staff in the company are rather more important than the money.'

'If you're in business, you must think of the profits,' I replied.

'That's true, but there has been an unfair situation going on vis-à-vis these two young people here.' (Peter points to the two Knight cards.) 'One of these has been paid more than the other and this is just not fair. I will soon have to plead the case of the other one.'

'The next card is the Queen of Swords, reversed, which shows me that even though you do try to sort the situation out on behalf of the young person in question, he will still be angry and have a sense of grievance.'

'I'm sure you're right.'

'There could be a bit of nastiness here, so you must be absolutely right and fair, you must be absolutely honest and *you* must not make promises which you are in no position to keep.

'I'm expecting the Priestess to show up soon, it has to be one of the next two cards. Let's see.' (I turn the next card over.) 'Here it is! The Priestess, would you believe it — in this case reversed. You must learn from this: it is going to come out slightly badly, there may be promises unfulfilled, the young man will be used rather badly due to the "wheels within wheels" factor which you are not privileged to be able to see working. Don't fight too hard for his case, even if he *is* treated unfairly and leaves the job. This is *his* lesson in life, not yours. You have got to be seen as being something of a company man. This could go against your nature. You must use your sense of self-preservation and craftiness because I think this young man is going to be sacrificed on the alter of the King of Staves' stupidity.'

'That's absolutely right, yes, I can already foresee that happening. There will be a compromise situation which is not going to be satisfactory. That is already a strong possibility. I have had treatment of this kind myself in the past and have had to cope with it.'

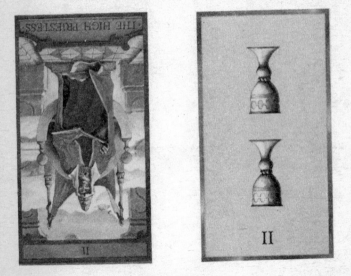

'The Priestess, reversed there, means that you mustn't make an emotional decision — there must be logic and the logic may well be political expediency. This may not be fair, but it is a matter of survival and no one is going to fight for *your* survival if you don't fight for yourself.

'The next card is the Two of Cups, reversed, and that is a parting. In other circumstances this could be the break-up of a relationship but, in this case, I think that any partings will be within the business context, although they will occur from an emotional standpoint. In plain English, if this man leaves, it will be because he is angry. The next card is the Lovers which is also reversed, and it seems that this situation which is brewing up, Peter, is going to have a lot of importance, out of all proportion to the matter in hand. How you handle this now is going to be important in the future. You are going to have to take a certain amount of criticism — unfair probably — but you must cope with it. Also you must make some sort of choice or decision and, with these two cards reversed, there is always the danger that you may make the wrong one.

'The last couple of cards are the Fool, reversed, and the Devil. The Devil binds you to your present choices and decisions for good, ill or otherwise, and even if you decided to get another job, you know that you would only find the same sort of decisions and situations waiting for you there. So you have got to make this choice and all other choices very carefully in the future; also you cannot discuss your problems with other people in the firm. You won't be able to discuss these decisions openly. The Fool, reversed, shows that this is not a time to make new starts or to make waves. When the Fool is upright you can step out and hope for the best, but with the reversal you have to hold back.

The reversed Lovers back there shows that other people in the group will make decisions which don't altogether suit you. You must walk a tightrope and be careful not to join any particular camp. Don't make any policy decisions which clash with official company thinking, even though you don't necessarily agree with it. This doesn't only apply to this issue, but also to other issues. You need to control your emotions. For some reason your instincts are working against you, and you must think with your head here not with your heart because so many emotional cards in the latter part of the layout are reversed. There will be problems to do with company policy and money. The Devil is a commitment and you have your own commitments to look to. Also the upright Devil means that you have to deal with the practicalities of a situation rather than the emotions.

Therefore, to recap on the reading, we have started with you doing a job which has given you a lot of joy and a chance to express yourself creatively in the past. Now you are being increasingly faced with the changeover to an executive, decision-making position. I think you are going to advance pretty rapidly now. You are also going to have to demand the money, position, type of office space, perks, etc., which will go with your increasing responsibilities.'

Peter commented, 'What you have shown me is very, very true, even down to describing the personalities of the people around me, but, more particularly, you have shown me the difficulty of my position now as a studio manager where I am the middle man between the upper levels and the lower ones who now treat me as being *their* manager.'

'You are being shot at by both sides. Remember the warning there against acting emotionally. I'll tell you something else; the fact that you and your wife both work for the firm draws a bit of jealousy towards you. Some people don't like it. They see that as something of a power base. I think on the whole that this year will be crucial for you: your firm is no more of a minefield than any other company, and you are pretty good at negotiating minefields. I think you will be, a year from now, not only older and wiser, more successful and more respected, but also more cynical and more disillusioned about people.'

Introduction to the Tree of Life Spread

Kabbalism (or Qabalism) is a framework of knowledge and understanding which, like astrology, takes many years of work and study to perfect. As I am an astrologer rather than a Kabbalist, I decided to ask my friend, Douglas Ashby, to contribute a few ideas to this section of the book. Douglas has spent many years teaching esoteric subjects including the Kabbala and, therefore, I felt quite safe in the knowledge that he could give a clear, concise and confident explanation of this deeply involved and specialized subject.

Reflections upon the Tree of Life by Douglas Ashby

A number of interesting special-purpose spreads utilize the structure of the Kabbalistic Tree of Life. The ten circles or spheres are called Sephiroth, which means 'emanations', and these, together with their twenty-two connecting paths, are said to reflect the way in which Creation takes place. Kabbala itself is said to be the inner Wisdom Tradition that lies behind both Judaism and Christianity, and whose roots can be found even further back. The structure of the Tree is an interesting one from the point of view of the Tarot as well, and a good deal of work was done by members of the magical Order of the Golden Dawn, at the turn of the century, on the relationship between the Tarot cards and the Tree.

1. There are twenty-two paths on the Tree and twenty-two cards in the Major Arcana.
2. There are ten Sephiroth and ten numbered cards in each suit.
3. There are four worlds or primary levels of existence in Kabbalistic teachings, and four suits as well as four Court cards.
4. With the addition of the notional Sephirah Daath (the dotted circle in the diagram) which translates as 'knowledge' and which is said to represent the essence of one's experience, we have a total of eleven, and then the Major Arcana fits on to the Tree exactly with two cards per Sephirah (singular of Sephiroth).

It is worth noting that, in some Tarot decks, there are two masculine Court cards — the King and the Knight — and two feminine Court cards — the Queen and Princess.

When relating the Tarot in this way, some other attributes are often utilized, such as the ancient four elements, viz:

Fire = Spirit = Staves = Active
Water = Emotions = Cups = Receptive
Air = Thoughts = Swords = Active
Earth = Physical manifestation = Coins = Receptive

The four Court cards in each suit are then seen as also representing the four elements in various combinations, i.e.:

Suit of Staves

King	*Queen*	*Knight*	*Page*
Fire of Fire	Water of Fire	Air of Fire	Earth of Fire

Suit of Cups

King	*Queen*	*Knight*	*Page*
Fire of Water	Water of Water	Air of Water	Earth of Water

Suit of Swords

King	Queen	Knight	Page
Fire of Air	Water of Air	Air of Air	Earth of Air

Suit of Coins

King	Queen	Knight	Page
Fire of Earth	Water of Earth	Air of Earth	Earth of Earth

An understanding of the nature of the elements and the suits then provides us with another way of looking at the Court cards that can be quite useful.

Description of the Tree of Life

The names shown on the diagram are the traditional Hebrew ones, and the descriptions given below are only a few of the many different attributes allocated to each of the Sephiroth. These will suffice for our present purposes, though.

Kether Spiritual impulse, higher self, spiritual influences surrounding one, the roots of new things due to come into one's life. Conception of anything.
The four Aces.

'Hokma Male image, how one relates to the active male force, new things beginning to come into being. Left side of the head. First month of pregnancy. Father.
The four Twos.

Binah Feminine image, how one relates to the receptive, structuring processes of life, right side of the head, second month of pregnancy. Mother.
The four Threes.

'Hesed Ideals, the law, religious matters, one's inner will, planning processes, compassionate nature, left shoulder and arm, third month of pregnancy. Female relatives.
The four Fours.

Geburah Active aspirations, ability to act, determination, strength,

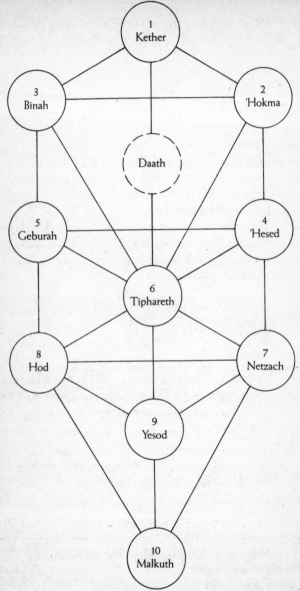

ability to destroy the past in order to create the future, right shoulder and arm, fourth month of pregnancy. Male relatives.
The four Fives.

Tiphareth Control, balance, harmony, heart centre, centre of being, lungs, solar plexus, active will, things now definitely in the process of coming to fruition. The fifth month of pregnancy. Husband in female reading.
The four Sixes.

Netzach Emotional nature, feelings, desires, artistic creativity, romance, left hand and hip-back-loin, sons, the sixth month of pregnancy.
The four Sevens.

Hod Thoughts, communication, speech, logic, right hand and hip-back-loins, sons, the seventh month of pregnancy.
The four Eights.

Yesod Imagination, instincts, habit patterns, sex, food, home environment, sexual organs. Eighth month of pregnancy. Wife in a male reading.
The four Nines.

Malkuth General physical condition and environment, what is happening now and just past, legs and feet. All things which have now come into manifestation or which are passing away. The ninth month of pregnancy. Birth and death.
The four Tens.

Tree of Life Reading by Douglas Ashby

As with all spreads it is important to decide in advance just what it is that you intend doing, and especially so here, as the Tree spread can be used in several different ways. In general it is laid down from the bottom (Malkuth) upwards (to Kether) in the reverse order of the numbers shown on the diagram. The latter show the sequence in which things come into manifestation but, when laying out the cards, the first card represents that which is already manifest. This is not hard

1.

11.

3.

5.

8.

6.

9.

10.

2.

4.

7.

to understand when you think of other spreads where the first card(s) laid represent past conditions. The cards are therefore laid up the Tree and are then read in the same order.

An individual Tree of Life spread can be used to obtain information about a specific problem or condition, or to obtain a current psychological profile of someone, for example. The cards are shuffled by the Questioner in the usual way and they are asked to think about the question they wish answered while doing so.

Here is an example of a reading for someone called Susan who was contemplating setting up a meditation group and wanted to know if this would be a good thing for her to do.

10.	Malkuth	Nine of Staves
9.	Yesed	Seven of Coins
8.	Hod	Eight of Swords
7.	Netzach	The Star
6.	Tiphareth	The Chariot
5.	Geburah	Strength
4.	'Hesed	The Hermit
3.	Binah	King of Coins
2.	'Hokma	King of Staves
1.	Kether	Seven of Cups
11.	Daath	Four of Cups

The reading

Position 10: Malkuth
The Nine of Staves: Known as the Lord of Great Strength, this is an excellent card to have in any position and suggests great success in the venture, though it will require application of energy to make it happen and there will be a certain amount of apprehension and fear about it beforehand. It suggests that Susan has the necessary strength and energy at the present time to undertake the leadership of such a group.

Position 9: Yesod
The Seven of Coins: Known as the Lord of Success Unfulfilled, this

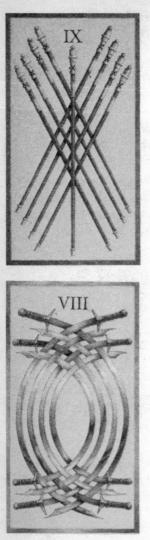

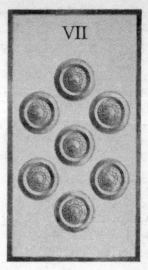

card suggests that from a monetary point of view the venture is unlikely
to be particularly rewarding, although it may also reflect Susan's own
uncertainty about how much to charge. As with all the Sevens, the

result will be very dependent upon the action taken, and so any uncertainties she has will be reflected in the result.

Position 8: Hod

The Eight of Swords: The Lord of Shortened Force. Being an Eight, this card goes naturally in this particular position, and says that she will have to be careful not to concentrate too much on detail at the expense of principles and more important things. The important thing will be to keep the right outlook on what she intends doing and not to expend all her energy on worrying about small points of detail.

Position 7: Netzach

The Star: The first of the four Major Arcana cards in the spread, the Star represents the guiding force of love and shows that Susan will be able to bring this to bear through her own outflowing emotional nature. The card also represents inner guidance available to her if she chooses to accept it.

Position 6: Tiphareth

The Chariot: The second of the Major Arcana cards, this one represents the spirit controlling and guiding the lower self. Placed in the central position of the tree, it suggests that Susan has now reached the point where she is capable of guiding others, having gained a degree of control over herself. While of itself this card does not necessarily indicate success, it does say that the conditions for success are present.

Position 5: *Geburah*

Strength: Another Major Arcana card and one very appropriate to this position. It indicates courage, strength, energy and spiritual strength, and shows that she *has* the necessary spiritual strength and proper aspiration to undertake such a venture. She should be able to bring the right blend of authority and helpfulness to the task she is contemplating.

Position 4: *Hesed*

The Hermit: The fourth of the Major Arcana cards, the Hermit denotes a teacher of hidden things, one who holds up his lamp as a guiding light for others. The Hermit is also one who is in retreat from the world, for a period at least, and also denotes caution, silence and patience. As this position has to do with planning, spiritual matters and so forth, it suggests that Susan needs to spend some time contemplating what she wishes to do so as to ensure that she approaches it with the right spiritual outlook. It also relates to guidance again, and she should not ignore the availability of this, whether in an inward sense or outwardly from others.

KING OF COINS   KING OF STAVES

Position 3: *Binah*
King of Coins: Here we have a masculine card in a feminine position, and one that rules the fundamental structure of things. Its placement here suggests that Susan sees this as something she wants to set about on her own, to be both initiator and executor of. Being Coins, it shows she has a good practical outlook on the venture. There is also a suggestion here that she sees it as a means of helping her husband out with the family income, albeit in a modest way. This is a card of increase and of steadiness and reliability, all of which suggests that she will approach the venture in a sensible way.

Position 2: *Hokma*
King of Staves: Placed appropriately in the active male position, this card shows that Susan has the necessary energy and spiritual strength

to undertake something of this sort properly. It also suggests, though, that assistance could be available to her from a man of a fiery nature who is already a teacher of some kind, someone who perhaps already occupies a position of trust in her spiritual life and whom she looks up to.

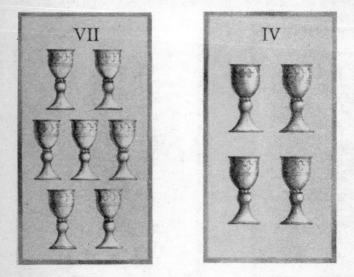

Position 1: Kether
The Seven of Cups: Called the Lord of Illusionary Success, this card says that success is possible, but could be lost through insufficient activity and/or a failure to follow up the idea properly. This would bring about disappointment, which is the general meaning of this card. There is also an element of deception about this card and, bearing in mind that it appears in the Kether position, there is a warning here for Susan not to be doing it simply for her own reasons or desires. (The Sevens all relate to Netzach and, therefore, to pleasure of one kind or another, as well as to creativity.)

Position 11: Daath
The Four of Cups: This card denotes the overall tone of the spread and what she can gain out of the venture in terms of pleasure and experience. This card is called the Lord of Blended Pleasure and suggests

a certain amount of discomfort and anxiety, as well as a degree of success and pleasure gained from it. She will need to watch that her own emotions do not get in the way of doing what she is setting out to do properly. The card is also one which suggests that this will not be a long-term affair but that, for as long as it does last, Susan will get pleasure out of it.

So far as the future is concerned, we shall have to wait to see the outcome, but Susan agreed that she was uncertain about how much to charge (see position 9) as this was her first attempt at something like this. She added that she did not expect it to bring in much in the way of income, but anything which it did bring in would be useful.

CHAPTER ELEVEN

Using the Same Spread in Two Different Ways

This reading demonstrates how one layout can sometimes be used in two different ways. I asked Judy to shuffle, cut and then to choose thirteen cards. We then laid these cards out in a circle starting at the left-hand side and going *anti-clockwise*. I did the reading firstly as an annual one and then went round the same cards again for an astrological reading. The card positions are numbered from one to twelve with one in the middle for luck. The specific meanings of each astrological house position can be found on pages 166-9. After completing this experiment, I decided that the idea would probably have worked better the other way round, ie, the astrological reading first with the annual one done afterwards. However, I have reproduced the reading just as it happened so that you can judge for yourself how it worked out. Incidentally, I did not choose a significator, although I could see Judy as the Queen of Cups. As it happens the Queen didn't show up in the reading at all. I used both upright and reversed cards in this reading.

Judy

I've known Judy for years — in fact she gave me tips on Tarot reading when I was at the learning stage myself. Judy is not a professional Tarot Reader but a very gifted amateur. She sees the cards in a slightly different way from me and puts a great deal of intuition into her readings, just as I do. The amount of clairvoyance and intuition that can be brought to a reading depends upon a number of factors. Firstly, the Reader has to be in a reasonably relaxed frame of mind — tiredness or even being slightly under the effects of alcohol can actually make one *more* intuitive as the logical side of the mind is slightly muted. It is far easier to receive psychic impressions if your Questioner is also psychic, because a kind of to-and-fro effect then occurs.

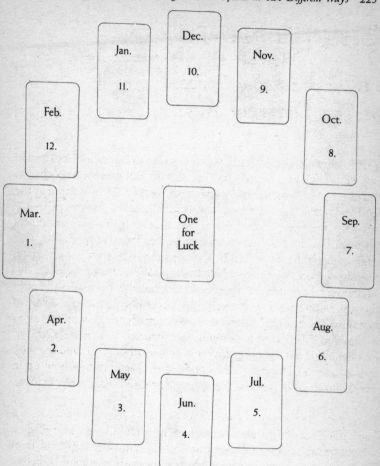

Judy is a small brunette who manages to be both slim and curvy at the same time; she lives in a flat with her two lovely daughters Rebecca and Anna. She is the head of a section in a large store and is currently nearing the end of a course of studies which will enable her to work as a psychotherapist. Judy has quite a few interests, both intellectual and artistic, and is good company for a 'girls' night out'.

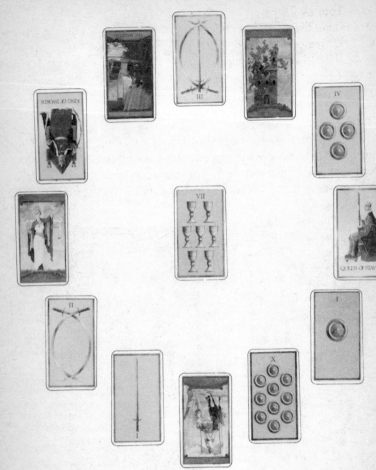

1.   Justice
2.   Two of Swords
3.   Ace of Swords, reversed
4.   The Chariot, reversed
5.   Ten of Coins
6.   Ace of Coins
7.   Queen of Staves

8.   Four of Coins
9.   The Tower
10. Three of Swords, reversed
11. The Magician, reversed
12. King of Swords, reversed
One for luck — Seven of Cups

The Annual Spread reading
'The one-for-luck card is the Seven of Cups which suggests that there could be many roads open to you this year, lots of choices. You probably don't yet know which way to go, but you could actually find the right pathway soon, if not you will have to continue to experiment for a while longer.'

March (we did this reading early in the month of March)
'This is the Justice card. This shows legal dealings, papers to sign, a contract for work maybe. You could be involved with someone else's papers in a way. You are weighing up a couple of ideas and trying to create a balance in your life, looking back towards the Seven card at the variety of options shown there.'

April

'Two of Swords, that's curious isn't it?' asked Judy.

'Another weighing up card but no real change in your life as yet, because this card shows that things are static. You can't really do very much to change your situation, you can't see your way forward yet.'

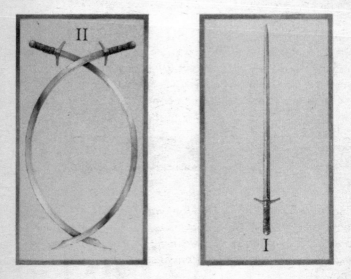

May

'The Ace of Swords, reversed, could be dental or medical treatment, even an injection. This also tells me that, although you are becoming increasingly frustrated, you will have to remember that this is a very powerful card which, when reversed, implies that you will need to exert a certain amount of self-control. Perhaps a cautious move forward might be indicated now.'

June

'The Chariot, reversed. Well on a very silly level, this means problems with the car or problems regarding overseas travel. On a deeper level still, the inner and outer sides of your personality are not working harmoniously together. You could be rushing around rather pointlessly.'

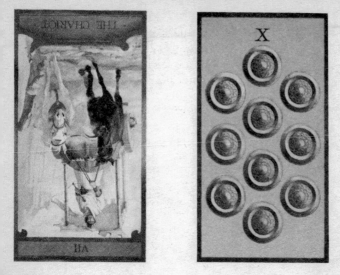

July
'This one is the Ten of Coins, therefore you could receive a raise in salary now giving you not only enough for essentials but also something over for treats. Some kind of roots are being put down now. The basis of a long-lasting and very good system of some kind is beginning to occur now.'

August
'Ace of Coins. I often see this coming up when people opt for self-employment. It certainly means making use of your talents. There could be a raise in salary, a bonus, even a win! A far better financial situation, also something rooted and very good. A wise move and also a fresh start financially.

'Judy, as I write this down, I feel something is going to happen regarding the people who are leasing your house — there may be some sort of change in your favour there.'

September
'The Queen of Staves — this could be a joint venture with another female; she will probably be slim, active and businesslike. This could

QUEEN OF STAVES

be a business venture of your own as it's such a fiery card which invests you with the faith, hope and optimism necessary for a new venture. This Queen is not calculating like the Queen of Coins, she is essentially energetic and optimistic.'

October
'The next card is the Four of Coins which implies material security, material gain. I still get the strong feeling that you are about to begin a more lucrative phase of your life now. You seem to be starting something interesting.'

November
'Now we have the Tower. Most people who know Tarot fear this card because it so often brings a sudden shock. However, it is sometimes associated with the home, the fabric of the home, that is. The worst that I see happening is something like a flood, fire or a break-in at your home. So it might be a good idea, while you've got money coming in, to take out some insurance for the home. The other thing about the Tower is that it brings enlightenment: it might bring a shock but it wakes you up and makes you change your outlook and break free from old habit patterns.'

December
'You have had very few reversed cards here, but here is the Three of Swords, reversed; this card is actually better if it's reversed. It's a sad

card and it probably shows that once again, Christmas is going to be a fairly lonely time — it's not your time of the year.'

Judy commented here that she had never had a good Christmas, that it was always a bad time of the year for her.

'Well, this one will not be the exception, but it is not disastrous. Sorry about this but I'm getting a clairvoyant flash. Have you got any parents alive, Judy?'

'Yes, my father.'

'I've got the feeling that you could be rushing him into hospital at that time. However, this card does have a slightly optimistic side if it's reversed, and that is to tell me that most of your heartbreak, heartache, etc., is over with, it's slipping backwards into the past. This card shows the end of misery and heartbreak.'

January

'The Magician, reversed. I find myself wanting to give you a warning: there could be some trickery associated with this new venture, just be careful.'

Judy picked up the card and said, 'The Magician has always meant a man, an important man in my life.'

'Fair enough, but be careful because, when this card is reversed, there is something missing. It's as if you've only got half the truth. This is supposed to represent a confidence artist, therefore things may not be as they seem.

February
'Finally we have the King of Swords, reversed. Yes, there does seem to be a new man, but also there could be a connection with hospitals, or with the law. There could well be some kind of awkwardness or misunderstanding. If this *is* to be a new man in your life, he will be dark-haired, very astute, bright and well-qualified professionally.'

The Astrological Spread reading

Position 1: Justice
'You are still seen here trying to weigh things up and trying to create balance in your life. I am still picking up something important in a legal way in this reading.

Position 2: Two of Swords
'This shows your resources and finances: they are not going to alter at the moment, they are steady.'

Position 3: Ace of Swords, reversed
'Don't impose too much on others or allow others to impose too much on you. The car could need attention now, perhaps the exhaust pipe is falling off.'

Judy broke in, 'Funny you should say that, the exhaust pipe *is* falling off.'

'To be honest, I'm not sure whether I'm reading the cards alone now or just reading you.'

Position 4: The Chariot, reversed
'This card is placed in the home area and means that you will have difficulties in coping with something at home. You are going to have more dealings with your father, therefore you could be driving back and forth between his home and your own and coping with him as well as giving attention to matters at your own home.'

Position 5: Ten of Coins
'This is supposed to be the fun area of the spread, but this is such a solid and respectable card that I am inclined to think that this concerns your psychology studies.'

Position 6: Ace of Coins
'This card is in the area of work and it tells me that there should be a bonus, raise or even an extra form of income from self-employment.'

Position 7: Queen of Staves
'This looks even more like a partnership with a woman now, a businesslike woman. There will be someone helping you in a practical way soon.'

Position 8: Four of Coins
'Somebody is going to be providing you with the means of security — you may do your psychology work in your spare time as well as

remain at work for the moment. There will soon be mature and sensible people around to help you.'

Position 9: *The Tower*
'If you *must* pick this card, this is about the least harmful place in which to find it because this is a particularly impersonal position in the spread. This looks like some sort of trip which doesn't work out. This position occasionally refers to a second marriage, so your "ex" will suddenly emerge from the woodwork. There could be something to do with a foreigner, or even the law in some way. It seems to be a shock from outside rather than from within, and I feel that the circumstances will work out well for you in the long run.'

Position 10: *Three of Swords, reversed*
'This is the end of a lot of sadness and loss, you will know much more clearly by the end of this year where you are headed. I think you are aiming to be a little less vulnerable too, less vulnerable to financial and emotional problems.'

Position 11: *The Magician, reversed*
'There are one or two tricky people around you who do not want to tell you the whole truth; they also make promises which they can't or won't keep. There is a slight indication that you should keep your financial position under wraps now. Any new man in your life could have hidden problems, or will be in a funny frame of mind.'

Position 12: *King of Swords, reversed*
'This is something to do with your own unconscious mind. You may meet someone who disturbs you, without allowing yourself to admit that there could be a problem. I don't know, Judy, I may be making too much of this. There will also be something to do with doctors, lawyers and other professional people which hasn't come to light yet.'

After the reading
Judy said that she could relate to most of the reading. There *were* elderly people living in her property and it would be a blessing for her if they left. She could not envisage being completely self-employed, but could

begin to operate as a part-time psychotherapist in the future, although probably not within the coming year. She certainly did have a difficult man in the background of her life who seemed to fit the Magician and King of Swords type of nature.

Judy hoped that I was right about the raise or bonus. She said that her father seemed to be in good health at the moment but admitted that, where elderly people are concerned, one never knows. We both agreed that, all in all, this was a successful reading that could give a measure of guidance.

Postscript

Judy has now met her 'Magician' and moved to another part of the country. She is letting her house out to students and is hoping to begin work as a psychotherapist soon.

CHAPTER TWELVE

Conclusion

The readings in this book were collected during the winter of 1985/86. Those which concerned the Questioners' current states of affairs were judged to be accurate, and even some of the futuristic ones are now beginning to work out. The longer-term event readings have yet to materialize; time alone will tell how accurate they are — maybe I'll get a chance to let you in on the results in another book. I tried to find as diverse a group of people as possible, but the same old themes of relationships, money and work came up time and time again.

I tried to choose a variety of spreads and also to show, by repeating some of them, how a simple spread can be used in many different ways. Whilst researching this book, I must have looked at about forty different spreads. I rejected some because they were similar to those which I already had in the book, while others were too complicated. I tried to include some of the oldest ideas and some of the most modern. In short, there are many methods which I *could* have used but I have tried to show as wide a variation as possible of those ideas which a beginner or an improver could most easily cope with.

By writing a book like this, I have laid myself open to criticism of my methods of reading the cards. There are some clever people around who know the whole range of meanings related to each card backwards and forwards but, in the end, it's one's own feelings which have to be the guide. No amount of arcane knowledge, no beauty or dignity in the manner of expressing oneself can beat good old intuition and a down-to-earth approach.

Please take your own route to understanding the cards and use this book as a starting point. May your adventures with the Tarot bring you great good fortune.

FURTHER INFORMATION

The PREDICTION TAROT CARDS used to illustrate this book are
available from all good bookshops and tarot suppliers, or direct from:

THE AQUARIAN PRESS
Denington Estate
Wellingborough
Northamptonshire
NN8 2RQ

INDEX